Individually wrap squares of fudge in brightly colored cellophane.

Tie a stack of cookies with a pretty gingham ribbon.

Cookies & candy

Nestle bite-size cookies inside a decorative teacup before giving.

Fill take-out boxes with homemade cookies & candy.

Old-fashioned milk bottles are just right for holding bite-size candy.

Friendship Toffee Cookies in a Jar

A wonderful gift for birthdays, graduations or just because!

1 c. toffee chips
1/2 c. chopped pecans, toasted
   and cooled
1/2 c. dark brown sugar, packed
2 c. buttermilk biscuit baking
   mix, divided

1/2 c. light brown sugar, packed
1/2 t. salt
1 t. vanilla powder
1/2 c. chocolate chips

Layer first 3 ingredients in a one-quart, wide-mouth jar, packing tightly after each addition. Layer one cup biscuit baking mix, brown sugar, salt, vanilla powder and remaining biscuit baking mix on top. Fill remaining space with chocolate chips; secure lid and attach instructions.

Instructions:

Combine mix, 1/2 cup melted butter and one egg in a medium mixing bowl. Mix well. Shape dough into one-inch balls; arrange on greased baking sheets. Bake at 375 degrees until golden, about 10 to 12 minutes. Makes 2 to 3 dozen.

Top off Friendship Toffee Cookies in a Jar with a bright ribbon flower. Cut 5 strips of 6-inch long ribbon, then cut each end into a "V" shape. Stack the ribbons together and tie in the middle with a small wire. Thread floss through a button and tie to the center over the wire. Twist and spread the ribbons apart to make a round flower.

A Country Store In Your Mailbox®

Gooseberry Patch
600 London Road
Department Book
Delaware, OH 43015

1·800·854·6673
www.gooseberrypatch.com

Copyright 2003, Gooseberry Patch 1-931890-13-7
First Printing, July, 2003

How To Subscribe

Would you like to receive
"A Country Store in Your Mailbox"®?
For a 2-year subscription to our
Gooseberry Patch catalog, simply send $3.00 to:

Gooseberry Patch   600 London Road   Delaware, Ohio 43015

Contents

year 'round ideas!

Gather up all your stamps, stickers & glitter for gift tags.

Use mini clothespins to attach gift tags & instructions.

Use a tamper to pack jar layers tightly.

Cookie Mix

Pack gifts in boxes filled with popped popcorn before mailing.

Retro lunch boxes make clever containers for mixes.

*✦Dedication✦

For everyone with a generous heart who
loves delighting friends & family with
oh-so-clever gifts any time of the year.

Keep an eye out for vintage silver spoons at
flea markets & tie them onto a stack of cocoa
mixes, ice cream sauces or jams.

Cookies & Candy

Chocolate Crunchies

Make these goodies up to 3 months ahead of giving. Just layer cookies between sheets of wax paper in an airtight container and freeze.

4 1-oz. sqs. unsweetened
   baking chocolate
1/4 c. butter
4 eggs
2 c. sugar
2 t. almond extract

2 c. all-purpose flour
2 t. baking powder
1/2 t. salt
1/2 c. chopped almonds, toasted
1/2 c. powdered sugar

Melt chocolate and butter together in a double boiler; cool and pour into a mixing bowl. Blend in eggs, one at a time; gradually stir in sugar. Add almond extract. Set aside. Combine flour, baking powder and salt; mix into chocolate mixture. Fold in almonds; cover and chill dough for 2 hours. Shape dough into one-inch balls; roll in powdered sugar and arrange on lightly greased baking sheets. Bake at 300 degrees for 15 to 18 minutes; cool on wire racks. Makes about 5 dozen.

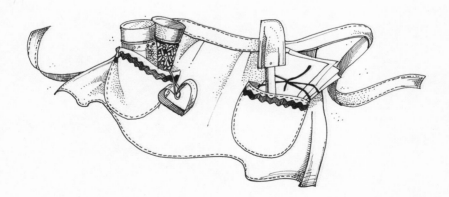

Make a gift basket for a beginning baker. Personalize a mini apron with fabric paint and fill the pockets with cookie cutters, a mini spatula, recipe cards and sprinkles...add it to a basket with a batch of homemade cookies for inspiration!

Spiced Cookie Mix

The softest crinkle cookies full of sugar & spice.

2 c. all-purpose flour
1 c. sugar
1 t. baking soda
1 t. baking powder

1/2 t. nutmeg
1/4 t. ground cloves
1/2 t. allspice
1 t. ground ginger

Combine ingredients in a large mixing bowl; mix well. Spoon into a large plastic zipping bag; seal and attach instructions.

Instructions:

Place one cup sugar in a small bowl; set aside. Cream 3/4 cup softened butter, one egg and 1/4 cup molasses; add cookie mix, blending until smooth. Shape dough into one-inch balls; roll each in sugar. Arrange 2 inches apart on ungreased baking sheets; bake at 375 degrees for 10 to 12 minutes. Cool on wire racks. Makes 4 dozen.

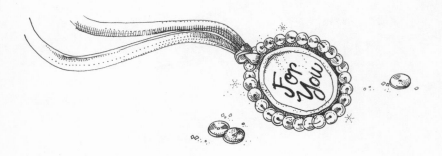

Metal-rimmed key tags make oh-so-clever gift tags.
Dress them up by covering the tag with glitter glue, then press a flat clear marble or gem in the center. Thread a shimmery ribbon through the tag and and tie onto a jar mix.

Cookies & Candy

Cinnamon & Sugar Sweetie Mix

Just like old-fashioned snickerdoodles.

2-3/4 c. all-purpose flour	2 t. cream of tartar
1/4 t. salt	1-1/2 c. sugar
1 t. baking soda	1 t. cinnamon

Combine ingredients; store in an airtight container. Attach instructions.

Instructions:

Combine 1/2 cup sugar and one tablespoon cinnamon in a small bowl; set aside. Cream one cup butter until light and fluffy; add 2 eggs. Blend in cookie mix; mix well. Shape dough into one-inch balls; roll in sugar-cinnamon mixture. Arrange 2 inches apart on ungreased baking sheets; bake at 350 degrees for 15 to 18 minutes. Cool on wire racks. Makes about 5 dozen.

Surprise a sweetie with a heartfelt gift! Wrap a bright pink ribbon around a container of Cinnamon & Sugar Sweetie Mix and tie in a bow. Cut out 4 heart shapes from coordinating felt and glue 2 to each ribbon end, sandwiching the ribbon in between the hearts...too cute!

Coconut Whispers

Friends will be standing in line for these sugar-dusted cookies.

1 c. butter
1 c. sugar
1 egg
1 t. vanilla extract
1 t. almond extract

2-1/4 c. all-purpose flour
1/2 t. baking soda
1/2 t. salt
2 c. flaked coconut
Garnish: sugar

Cream butter and sugar; add egg and extracts. In a separate mixing bowl, mix flour, baking soda and salt together; gradually blend into egg mixture. Fold in coconut. Drop dough by heaping tablespoonfuls onto parchment paper-lined baking sheets. Sprinkle each cookie with additional sugar; press with the bottom of a sugar-coated glass to flatten slightly. Bake at 325 degrees for 12 to 15 minutes; cool on a wire rack. Makes 3 to 4 dozen.

Add a personal touch to a gift in minutes with letter beads. Wrap a wide ribbon around a wrapped box of cookies, securing ends in back with tape. Thread letter beads onto narrow ribbon to spell out a name, and layer over the wide ribbon, knotting in back.

Cookies & Candy

White Chocolate-Macadamia Cookies in a Jar

With their rich flavor and buttery texture, macadamia nuts turn these cookies into a supreme dessert.

1/2 c. macadamia pieces
1/2 c. white chocolate chips
1/2 c. light brown sugar, packed

2 c. buttermilk biscuit baking mix, divided
1/2 c. dark brown sugar, packed

Layer first three ingredients in a one-quart, wide-mouth jar, firmly packing after each addition. Layer one cup biscuit baking mix, dark brown sugar and remaining biscuit baking mix; add more chopped macadamia nuts or white chocolate chips to any remaining space. Secure lid and attach instructions.

Instructions:

Pour mix into a medium mixing bowl; add 1/2 cup melted butter, one egg and one teaspoon vanilla extract. Mix well. Shape dough into one-inch balls; arrange on greased baking sheets. Bake at 375 degrees until golden, about 10 to 12 minutes. Makes 2-1/2 dozen.

Small brown paper sacks or coin envelopes make clever totes for mixing instructions. Print a greeting and baking instructions on separate pieces of cardstock. Glue the greeting to the front of the bag and slip the instructions inside. Punch a pair of holes in the top of the bag and tie it to a jar mix with jute.

Old-Fashioned Sweet Sponge Candy

A melt-in-your-mouth favorite.

1 c. sugar
1 T. white vinegar

1 c. corn syrup
1 T. baking soda

Line the bottom and sides of a 9"x9" baking pan with aluminum foil;
butter aluminum foil and set aside. Combine sugar, vinegar and corn
syrup in a heavy saucepan; stir over medium heat until sugar
dissolves. Heat until mixture reaches the hard-crack stage, or 290 to
310 degrees on a candy thermometer; remove from heat. Carefully stir
in baking soda; mixture will foam up quite high. Pour mixture into
prepared pan; set aside at room temperature until firm. Invert pan to
remove candy; peel foil from back. Break candy into small pieces;
store in an airtight container. Makes about 1/2 pound.

Butterscotch Candy

Looking for a sweet treat? This will hit the spot!

2 c. sugar
1/4 c. butter

1/4 c. water
1 T. white vinegar

Combine ingredients in a heavy saucepan; heat over medium heat
until mixture reaches the soft-crack stage, or 270 to 289 degrees on a
candy thermometer. Pour into a buttered jelly-roll pan; set aside to
cool. Cut into squares to serve. Makes about one pound.

Wrap individual squares of Butterscotch Candy and
Old-Fashioned Sweet Sponge Candy in wax paper and give in a
jadite glass bowl...sure to bring back memories
of Mom's kitchen.

Cookies & Candy

Celebration Cookie Sticks

Let little hands do the decorating.

1-1/2 c. powdered sugar
1 c. butter, softened
.14-oz. pkg. unsweetened
   strawberry drink mix
1 t. vanilla extract
1 egg

2-3/4 c. all-purpose flour
1 t. cream of tartar
16-oz. container vanilla frosting
Garnish: assorted jimmies and
   colored sugars

Combine first 5 ingredients; mix well. Stir in flour and cream of tartar; cover and refrigerate dough for at least 30 minutes. Divide dough into 20 pieces; use floured hands to roll each into a 6-inch log on a lightly floured surface. Arrange 2 inches apart on ungreased baking sheets; bake at 375 degrees for 8 to 10 minutes. Cool for 2 minutes; remove to wire racks to cool completely, about 30 minutes. Spread the top third of each cookie stick with frosting; sprinkle with jimmies or colored sugars. Makes 20.

Handy party favors! Nestle groups of Celebration Cookie Sticks inside colorful party hats. Arrange the hats in a glass bowl and let guests pick one up on their way out.

Powder Puff Cookie Mix

Bite-size favorites that neighbors and friends will love!

1/2 c. powdered sugar   1 c. chopped walnuts
2-1/3 c. all-purpose flour

Combine powdered sugar and flour; spoon into an airtight container.
Layer walnuts on top; secure lid. Attach instructions.

Instructions:

Cream 3/4 cup shortening and 1/4 cup softened butter together; stir
in 2 teaspoons vanilla extract. Blend in cookie mix. Shape dough into
one-inch balls and arrange on greased baking sheets. Bake at
325 degrees for 20 to 25 minutes; cool slightly. Place one cup
powdered sugar in a small bowl; roll cookies in sugar while warm.
Makes 4 dozen.

Be prepared ahead of time with gifts for friends who drop by
during the holidays or special occasions. Cookie and beverage
mixes are great to store in the pantry for up to 6 months and
cookie cutters with favorite recipes attached are simple,
heartfelt gifts to keep on hand all year.

Cookies & Candy

Peanut Butter Criss-Cross Cookies in a Jar

Crunchy nuts, creamy peanut butter and chewy chocolate...the best combination.

1-1/2 c. all-purpose flour
1 t. baking soda
1/2 t. salt
3/4 c. mini chocolate chips

3/4 c. chopped peanuts
3/4 c. brown sugar, packed
3/4 c. sugar

Combine flour, baking soda and salt together; set aside. Pressing firmly between additions, layer chocolate chips, peanuts, flour mixture, brown sugar and sugar in a one-quart, wide-mouth jar. Secure lid and attach instructions.

Instructions:

Empty cookie mix into a large mixing bowl; stir to combine. Add 1/2 cup softened butter, 1/2 cup creamy peanut butter, one beaten egg and 2 teaspoons vanilla extract; mix well. Drop by tablespoonfuls onto greased baking sheets; flatten slightly with fork tines. Bake at 350 degrees for 10 to 12 minutes. Cool for 5 minutes; remove to wire rack to cool completely. Makes about 3 dozen.

Peanut Butter Criss-Cross Cookies

Empty cookie mix into a large mixing bowl; stir to combine. Add ½ c. softened butter, ½ c. peanut butter, 1 beaten egg & 2 t. vanilla extract; mix well. Drop by tablespoonfuls onto greased baking sheets, flatten slightly with fork tines. Bake at 350° for 10-12 minutes. * Cool for 5 minutes; remove to wire rack to cool completely. Makes 3 dozen.

Here's your instruction tag to copy & tie on.

Snowcap Cookies

*These look just like mini mountain peaks and are a great
make-ahead gift because they freeze so well.*

3/4 c. butter, softened
1 c. sugar
3 eggs
1 t. vanilla extract
6 1-oz. sqs. white baking
   chocolate, melted and cooled
3-1/2 c. all-purpose flour

1 t. baking powder
1 t. salt
1/8 t. nutmeg
1-1/2 c. chopped walnuts,
   toasted
Garnish: powdered sugar

Cream butter and sugar until light and fluffy; add eggs, one at a time, mixing well after each addition. Stir in vanilla; add melted chocolate, blending for 30 seconds. Set mixture aside. Combine flour, baking powder, salt and nutmeg together; gradually add to butter mixture. Fold in walnuts. Drop by tablespoonfuls onto greased baking sheets. Bake at 350 degrees for 10 to 12 minutes; cool on wire racks. Sprinkle tops with powdered sugar. Makes 3 to 4 dozen.

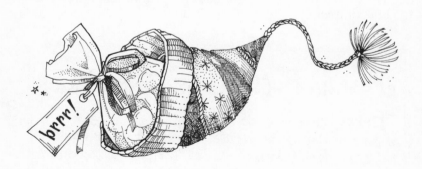

Snowcaps in a snow cap! Wrap a batch of
Snowcap Cookies in clear plastic wrap, then tuck inside a
woolly toboggan...add a package of cocoa mix to really
chase the chills away.

Cookies & Candy

Prize-Winning Chocolate Chip Cookies

A quick recipe that is a welcome delight for any family.

3 c. all-purpose flour
1 t. baking soda
1-1/2 t. salt
1 c. margarine
1-1/3 c. sugar

2/3 c. brown sugar, packed
2 t. vanilla extract
2 eggs
3 c. semi-sweet chocolate chips

Combine flour, baking soda and salt; set aside. Cream margarine and sugars in a large mixing bowl until light; blend in vanilla and eggs until smooth. Gradually mix in dry ingredients; fold in chocolate chips. Drop by heaping tablespoonfuls about 3 inches apart onto parchment paper-lined baking sheets; bake at 325 degrees for 10 to 12 minutes. Makes about 4 dozen.

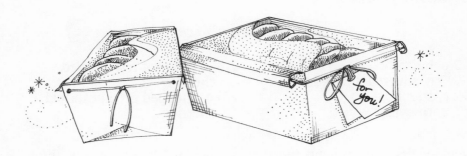

Signed, sealed and delivered! Line up homemade cookies inside a small cardboard box (about the size of a mini loaf pan), run a glue stick along the box edges and place a sheet of clear cellophane over top. Allow glue to dry and trim cellophane edges. Cookies stay fresh and the package is oh-so sweet!

Never-Fail Caramels

A tried & true favorite.

2 c. sugar
1 c. brown sugar, packed
1 c. corn syrup
1 c. evaporated milk

2 c. whipping cream
1 c. butter
1-1/2 t. vanilla extract

Combine all ingredients, except vanilla, in a heavy saucepan. Stirring constantly, heat mixture until caramel reaches the firm-ball stage, or 244 to 249 degrees on a candy thermometer. Remove from heat and stir in vanilla. Pour mixture into a buttered jelly-roll pan; cool. Cut caramel into small squares and wrap individually in wax paper. Makes 4 to 5 dozen.

Almond Jewels

Almost too pretty to eat!

1/2 c. butter
1-2/3 c. slivered almonds
1/2 c. sugar
2 T. corn syrup

1/3 c. chopped red candied
 cherries
1/3 c. chopped green candied
 cherries

Combine first 4 ingredients together in a heavy 10" skillet; sauté until almonds and sugar are golden. Remove from heat; sprinkle with cherries, without stirring. Drop by tablespoonfuls onto wax paper-lined baking sheets; refrigerate until firm. Store in an airtight container at room temperature. Makes about 2-1/2 dozen.

Dress up a holiday cookie tray in no time!
Place individual clusters of Almond Jewels in bright
green or red foil candy cups.

Cookies & Candy

Nutty Maple Candy

Cut into leaves with mini cookie cutters for a fall celebration.

12-oz. pkg. chocolate chips
12-oz. pkg. butterscotch chips
12-oz. jar creamy peanut butter
1 c. butter
1/2 c. evaporated milk

3-oz. pkg. cook & serve vanilla
   pudding mix
1-1/2 T. maple flavoring
2 t. vanilla extract
2-lb. pkg. powdered sugar
3 c. chopped peanuts

Melt chocolate and butterscotch chips together in a double boiler; add peanut butter, stirring until smooth. Spread 1-3/4 cups mixture into a buttered jelly-roll pan; refrigerate until firm. Set remaining mixture aside. Melt butter in a heavy saucepan; stir in milk and pudding mix. Heat over medium heat until thickened; remove from heat. Add maple flavoring and vanilla; stir in powdered sugar. Spread over chilled chocolate mixture; return to refrigerator. Re-melt, if necessary, remaining chocolate mixture in saucepan; stir in peanuts. Carefully spread over pudding mixture; refrigerate until firm. Cut into squares to serve. Makes about 5 dozen.

Surprise friends and co-workers with a falltime treat.
Arrange several squares of Nutty Maple Candy on mismatched
saucers and wrap them up with fall-colored cellophane.
Press maple leaves, write on them with a paint pen and
tie onto cellophane for gift tags.

Chocolate Pretzels

Try dipping the pretzels in finely chopped nuts too.

3/4 c. butter, softened
3/4 c. sugar
1 egg
1 t. vanilla extract
2 c. all-purpose flour

1/3 c. baking cocoa
2 t. baking powder
1 t. salt
Garnish: assorted sprinkles

Cream butter and sugar until light and fluffy; blend in egg and vanilla. Add flour, cocoa, baking powder and salt until just blended; divide dough in half. Wrap one half in plastic wrap; set aside. Shape remaining dough by tablespoonfuls into 9-inch long ropes. Twist into pretzel shapes; lightly press into sprinkles. Arrange sprinkle-side up on lightly greased baking sheets; repeat with remaining dough. Bake at 350 degrees for 15 minutes; remove to a wire rack to cool completely. Makes about 3 dozen.

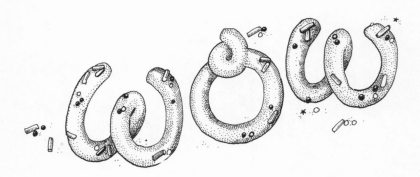

Easy as A-B-C! Instead of shaping Chocolate Pretzels into traditional pretzel shapes, form dough into letters...spell out names, "Congrats!" or "Celebrate!"

Cookies & Candy

Dazzling Neapolitan Cookies

These cookies only look difficult but are really easy to make.

1 c. butter, softened
1 c. sugar
1 egg
1 t. vanilla extract
2-1/2 c. all-purpose flour
1-1/2 t. baking powder
1/2 t. salt

1-oz. sq. baking chocolate, melted
1/3 c. chopped pecans
1/4 c. chopped candied cherries, diced
2 drops red food coloring
1/3 c. flaked coconut
1/2 t. almond extract

Cream butter and sugar until light and fluffy; add egg and vanilla. Gradually blend in flour, baking powder and salt; divide dough into thirds. Place each third in a separate mixing bowl. Stir chocolate and pecans into one third; set aside. Stir cherries and food coloring into another third; set aside. Stir coconut and almond extract into remaining third; set aside. Line an 8"x8" baking pan with plastic wrap; press chocolate dough evenly to cover the bottom of the pan. Layer with coconut mixture and then cherry mixture, pressing gently; cover and refrigerate for 8 hours. Lift dough from pan; cut into 5 equal sections. Carefully cut each section into 1/8-inch thick slices; arrange on ungreased baking sheets. Bake at 375 degrees for 8 to 10 minutes; remove to wire racks to cool. Makes 8 dozen.

Fill a pretty drinking glass with Dazzling Neapolitan Cookies, cover the top with a dainty handkerchief and secure with a ribbon...a delightful hostess gift.

Cute-as-a-Button Cookies in a Jar

Full of crunch and color.

3/4 c. sugar
1 c. quick-cooking oats,
    uncooked
1 c. candy-coated chocolates

3/4 c. brown sugar, packed
1-3/4 c. all-purpose flour
1 t. baking powder
1/2 t. baking soda

Layer sugar, oats, chocolates and brown sugar in a one-quart, wide-mouth jar; pack tightly. Mix together flour, baking powder and baking soda; add to jar. Secure lid and attach instructions.

Instructions:

Place cookie mix in a large bowl; blend in one egg and 1/2 cup softened butter. Mix well. Drop by teaspoonfuls onto lightly greased baking sheets. Bake at 350 degrees for 8 to 10 minutes. Makes about 5-1/2 dozen.

Keep an eye out at flea markets and craft stores for charming sewing boxes. Fill them with pretty ribbons, buttons, vintage fabric squares, new patterns and notions. Give with Cute-as-a-Button Cookies in a Jar with a button-shaped gift tag.

Cookies & Candy

It's Gotta Be Chocolate Cookies in a Jar

For the biggest chocolate fans on your gift list!

1/3 c. milk chocolate chips
1/3 c. white chocolate chips
1/3 c. semi-sweet chocolate
  chips
1/2 c. light brown sugar, packed

2 c. buttermilk biscuit baking
  mix, divided
1/2 t. salt
1/2 c. dark brown sugar, packed

Layer first 4 ingredients in a one-quart, wide-mouth jar in the order listed; add one cup biscuit baking mix and salt, packing firmly. Layer dark brown sugar and remaining biscuit baking mix; add additional chips to any remaining space. Secure lid and attach instructions.

Instructions:

Place cookie mix in a medium mixing bowl; stir to combine. Add 1/2 cup melted butter, one egg and one teaspoon vanilla extract; mix well. Shape dough into one-inch balls; arrange on greased baking sheets. Bake at 375 degrees for 10 to 12 minutes. Makes 2-1/2 dozen.

It doesn't take much to add cheer to simple wrapped gifts...just look around the house for fun accents like wooden spoons, cookie cutters, buttons, jingle bells, beads, greenery, seed packets, rubber stamps, confetti, dried flowers and cinnamon sticks.

Chocolate-Covered Peanut Clusters

Tastes like rocky road fudge!

2 12-oz. pkgs. semi-sweet
  chocolate chips
1 c. creamy peanut butter
16-oz. pkg. mini marshmallows

2-1/2 c. milk chocolate-covered
  peanuts
Garnish: powdered sugar

Melt chocolate chips with peanut butter in a double boiler; stir until smooth. Remove from heat; stir in marshmallows and chocolate-covered peanuts. Drop by tablespoonfuls onto a wax paper-lined baking sheet. Refrigerate until firm; sprinkle with powdered sugar before serving. Makes about 4 dozen.

Sugared Pecans

Make a batch of these for yourself to much on while wrapping gifts.

1 c. sugar
1-1/2 t. salt
1 t. cinnamon

1 egg white, room temperature
1 T. water
1-lb. pkg. pecan halves

Combine first 3 ingredients; set aside. Whisk egg white and water together until frothy; fold in pecan halves. Add sugar mixture; stir to coat pecans. Spread on an aluminum foil-lined baking sheet; bake at 300 degrees for 30 to 35 minutes. Remove from oven; separate pecans using a fork as they cool. Store in an airtight container. Makes about one pound.

Invite a few friends over and make a big batch of gift mixes
assembly-line style...everyone will go home with
gifts for giving!

Cookies & Candy

Marvelous Mocha Fudge

One piece of this rich fudge goes a long way!

1-1/2 c. sugar
2/3 c. evaporated milk
3 T. instant coffee granules
2 T. butter
1/4 t. salt

2 c. mini marshmallows
2 c. semi-sweet chocolate chips
1 t. vanilla extract
1/2 t. cinnamon

Combine first 5 ingredients in a heavy saucepan; bring to a full rolling boil over medium heat, stirring constantly. Boil and stir for 4 to 5 minutes; remove from heat. Mix in remaining ingredients; stir until marshmallows are melted. Pour into an 8"x8" baking pan lined with aluminum foil; refrigerate 2 to 3 hours until firm. Lift fudge from pan; remove foil and cut into squares. Makes 4 to 5 dozen.

Need to make a few gifts in a jiffy? Whip up a batch of Marvelous Mocha Fudge and pour it into mini Bundt® pans. Wrap each in cellophane, tie up with a ribbon and tuck a butter knife into the bow.

Red Hot Cinnamon Candy Popcorn

A unique recipe kids of all ages will love.

6 qts. popped popcorn
12-oz. pkg. red cinnamon
   candies
sugar

1 c. butter
1/2 c. corn syrup
1 t. salt
1/2 t. baking soda

Spread popcorn in a lightly buttered roasting pan; bake at 250 degrees
while preparing syrup. Pour cinnamon candies into a 2-cup measure;
fill remaining space to the top with sugar. Place in a heavy saucepan;
add butter, corn syrup and salt. Bring to a boil; boil for 5 minutes.
Remove from heat; carefully stir in baking soda. Pour over popcorn,
stirring to coat. Continue to bake at 250 degrees for one hour, stirring
every 15 minutes. Remove from oven; let cool. Break into pieces; store
in an airtight container. Makes 6 quarts.

Small paper punches come in all different shapes and they
add such so much fun to giftwrap. Wrap a package with plain
red paper, then cut a strip of white paper to use as a ribbon.
Cut a few shapes out of the white strip using punches
(hearts are so sweet!) and wrap the strip around the package,
taping in back. Red hearts will show through and the
cut-out white hearts can be glued on the package!

Cookies & Candy

Popcorn Candy Treats in a Jar

Know a busy mom? Give her this treat...she (and her kids) will thank you.

1/4 c. chopped pecans
1/2 c. doughnut-shaped oat
   cereal
1/2 c. peanuts
1-1/2 c. popped popcorn

1/2 c. bite-size crispy rice cereal
   squares
1/4 c. candy-coated chocolate
   mini-baking bits

Layer ingredients in a one-quart, wide-mouth jar; secure lid and attach instructions.

Instructions:

Spread popcorn mix in a lightly buttered roasting pan; set aside. Bring 1/4 cup packed brown sugar, 2 tablespoons butter and one tablespoon corn syrup to a boil in a heavy 3-quart saucepan; boil without stirring until mixture reaches the hard-ball stage, or 250 to 269 degrees on a candy thermometer, about 5 minutes. Remove from heat; stir in 1/4 teaspoon vanilla extract and 1/8 teaspoon baking soda. Pour over popcorn mix; stir to coat. Bake at 250 degrees for one hour, stirring every 15 minutes. Cool in pan; break apart. Store in an airtight container. Makes about one quart.

When preparing layered jar mixes,
be sure to firmly pack each layer.
Use a tamper, a large spoon or even
a small drinking glass to tightly
pack between layers...everything
will fit just right.

this   or this   or this

Cherry Cardamom Cookies

Sugar & spice and everything nice!

6-oz. jar maraschino cherries,
    drained and diced
2-1/3 c. plus 2 T. all-purpose
    flour, divided
1/2 c. butter, softened
1 c. sugar
3-oz. pkg. cream cheese,
    softened

1 egg
2 T. buttermilk
1 t. almond extract
1 t. cardamom
1 t. baking powder
1/2 t. baking soda
Garnish: powdered sugar

Toss cherries with 2 tablespoons flour; set aside. Cream butter, sugar and cream cheese until fluffy; blend in egg, buttermilk and almond extract. Gradually add in remaining flour, cardamom, baking powder and baking soda until just moistened; fold in cherry mixture. Shape dough into one-inch balls; arrange on ungreased baking sheets. Bake at 350 degrees for 12 to 14 minutes; remove to wire racks to cool completely. Sprinkle with powdered sugar when cool. Makes about 3 dozen.

Having friends over for lunch or dinner? Simple stacks of Cherry Cardamom Cookies tied up in a bow look charming at each place setting. Prop a card up against each stack to display guests' names, and print the recipe on the back.

Cookies & Candy

Polka-Dot Cherry Cookies in a Jar

Semi-sweet chocolate chips are just as tasty in these cookies.

3/4 c. sugar
1 c. all-purpose flour
1/2 t. baking powder
1/4 t. baking soda
1/4 t. salt

1 c. quick-cooking oats,
   uncooked
3/4 c. dried cherries
1/2 c. chopped walnuts
1 c. white chocolate chips

Layer sugar in a one-quart, wide-mouth jar; set aside. Combine
the next 4 ingredients together; add to jar, packing down gently.
Layer remaining ingredients in the order listed. Secure lid;
attach instructions.

Instructions:

Cream 1/2 cup butter in a large mixing bowl; add one egg. Blend in
cookie mix; mix well. Drop by teaspoonfuls onto greased baking
sheets; bake at 375 degrees for 10 to 12 minutes. Cool on a wire rack.
Makes about 3 dozen.

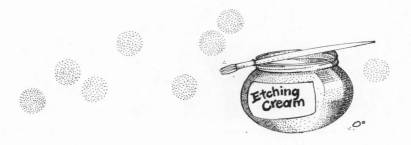

Lots of dots! Before filling a glass jar with ingredients for
Polka-Dot Cherry Cookies, add dots with etching cream. Just
arrange round stickers on the outside of the jar, paint with
2 coats of cream and let dry for 15 to 20 minutes. Wash and
dry jar, then peel off stickers...a frosted jar with clear dots.

Cinnamon Quilt Cookies

A baked cookie "blanket" sliced into squares.

3/4 c. butter, softened
1 c. sugar
1 egg yolk

2 c. all-purpose flour
1 T. cinnamon
3 c. pecans, finely chopped

Blend first 3 ingredients together with an electric mixer on medium speed for 2 to 3 minutes; add flour and cinnamon, mixing well. Roll dough out between 2 sheets of parchment paper to 1/8-inch thickness; remove top sheet of parchment. Invert dough onto a greased baking sheet; peel away remaining parchment paper. Sprinkle pecans evenly over the top; press gently into the dough. Bake at 350 degrees for 15 minutes; reduce heat to 250 degrees and continue baking for 10 minutes. Remove from oven; while hot slice into 3"x1-1/2" pieces with a pizza cutter. Cool completely on a wire rack. Makes about 3 dozen.

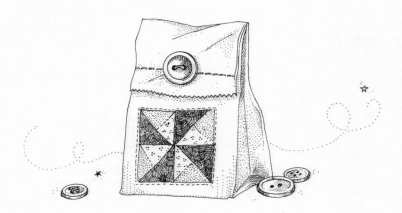

Handpaint a simple quilt design on the front of a white paper lunch bag and fill with Cinnamon Quilt Cookies. Fold the top over and sew a button in the middle to keep closed…"sew" easy!

Cookies & Candy

Brown-Eyed Susans

For fellow gardeners, add a few drops of yellow food coloring to the cookie dough for a bright wildflower color.

1 c. butter, softened
1/4 c. powdered sugar
2 t. vanilla extract

2 c. all-purpose flour
1/2 t. salt
48 whole almonds

Cream butter and powdered sugar until light and fluffy; blend in vanilla. Add flour and salt; mix well. Shape dough into one-inch balls; arrange on ungreased baking sheets. Flatten slightly with the bottom of a glass; bake at 350 degrees for 12 to 14 minutes. Cool completely on a wire rack; frost with frosting and top with an almond. Makes about 4 dozen.

Frosting:

1 c. powdered sugar
2 T. baking cocoa

2 T. hot water
1 t. vanilla extract

Combine powdered sugar and baking cocoa; mix well. Whisk in hot water and vanilla until smooth.

Set a few Brown-Eyed Susans inside several tiny terra cotta pots; fill other pots with mini bouquets and nestle all the pots in a vintage carrier...deliver to your garden club pals.

Lemon Slice Cookies

It just doesn't get any easier!

1 c. butter, softened
1 c. brown sugar, packed
1/2 c. sugar
1 egg
1 T. lemon zest

2 T. lemon juice
2 c. all-purpose flour
1/4 t. baking soda
1/2 t. salt

Cream butter and sugars together until light and fluffy; blend in egg, lemon zest and lemon juice. Add flour, baking soda and salt; mix until just blended. Divide dough in half; with floured hands, shape each half into a 10-inch long log. Wrap each in plastic wrap; refrigerate until firm. Wrap each roll in aluminum foil and again in printed fabric, if desired. Attach baking instructions to each roll. Makes 2 rolls.

Instructions:

Store dough in refrigerator until ready to bake. Cut chilled roll into 1/4-inch thick slices; arrange on greased baking sheets. Bake at 400 degrees for 8 to 10 minutes; cool on a wire rack. Makes about 3 dozen.

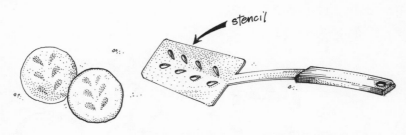

Spruce up Lemon Slice Cookies with whimsical patterns, found right in the kitchen. Use any utensil with a cut-out pattern...spatulas and potato mashers work great. Before baking, place the utensil on top of cookies and sprinkle colored sugar over top. Remove the utensil to show the cheery pattern.

Cookies & Candy

Fruity Cookies in a Jar

Colorful cereal gives this cookie mix a delightful flavor and crunch...and it looks so pretty layered in the jar.

1-1/4 c. all-purpose flour	2 c. fruit-flavored crispy rice
1/2 t. vanilla powder	cereal, divided
1/2 t. baking powder	2/3 c. brown sugar, packed
1/4 t. baking soda	1/2 t. salt
1/2 c. shortening	1/3 c. flaked coconut

Combine flour, vanilla powder, baking powder and baking soda; cut in shortening with a pastry blender until well blended. Layer one cup cereal, flour mixture, brown sugar, salt, remaining cereal and coconut in a one-quart, wide-mouth jar, packing tightly after each addition. Secure lid; attach instructions. Prepare within 6 weeks.

Instructions:

Pour cookie mix into a large mixing bowl; toss lightly to mix. Add one beaten egg and 2 tablespoons milk; mix well. Drop by rounded teaspoonfuls onto ungreased baking sheets; bake at 375 degrees for 8 to 9 minutes. Cool on baking sheets for one minute; transfer to wire racks to cool completely. Makes about 2 dozen.

A great welcome to out-of-town guests! Fill a basket with fresh fruits of the season...oranges, apples, pineapples, grapes, bananas or strawberries and include a mix of Fruity Cookies in a Jar.

County Fair Taffy

A old-fashioned favorite that's fun to give...and fun to make!

1 c. molasses	2 T. butter
1 c. sugar	1/8 t. salt
2 t. white vinegar	1/2 t. baking soda

Combine molasses, sugar and vinegar in a large saucepan; heat to the hard-ball stage, or 250 to 269 degrees on a candy thermometer. Remove from heat and stir in butter, salt and baking soda; continue stirring until foaming stops. Pour into a buttered 13"x9" baking pan; allow to cool. With buttered hands, pull taffy back and forth until taffy looses shine. Roll taffy into long ropes and cut into desired pieces with scissors. Wrap individually in wax paper. Makes 4 dozen.

Add a blue ribbon gift tag to a package of County Fair Taffy. Trim the ends of a length of blue ribbon into a "V" shape. Glue one end to the package, then make loops in decreasing sizes, gluing each crease to the package. Cut a circle out of blue cardstock for a label and glue over the crease.

Cookies & Candy

Sugar Cookie Cut-Outs

Want to pipe on frosting designs? Spoon frosting into a plastic zipping bag and snip one corner of the bag with scissors...an easy decorating bag without the clean-up.

1/3 c. butter, softened	1/8 t. salt
1/3 c. shortening	1 egg
3/4 c. sugar	1 t. vanilla extract
1 t. baking powder	2 c. all-purpose flour

Cream butter and shortening; add sugar, baking powder and salt. Blend in egg and vanilla; mix well. Gradually add flour; mix until dough is smooth. Divide dough in half; wrap each in plastic wrap and refrigerate for 3 hours. Roll dough out to 1/8-inch thickness on a lightly floured surface; cut into desired shapes using cookie cutters. Arrange on ungreased baking sheets; bake at 375 degrees for 6 to 8 minutes. Cool on wire racks; frost. Makes 3 to 4 dozen.

Powdered Sugar Frosting:

1 c. powdered sugar	milk
1/2 t. vanilla extract	Optional: desired food coloring

Combine powdered sugar, vanilla and one tablespoon milk; blend in additional milk, one teaspoon at a time, until desired spreading consistency is reached. Divide into several bowls; tint each with a different color food coloring, if desired.

Decorate a kitchen towel by sewing on buttons, rick-rack, ribbons and appliqué designs. Lay it in a wicker basket, add a batch of Sugar Cookie Cut-Outs and some fun cookie cutters.

Amazing Double Chocolate Truffles

*Try making flavored truffles by stirring in different extracts...a
teaspoon of peppermint, orange or raspberry extract will do the trick.*

6 1-oz. sqs. semi-sweet baking
   chocolate, chopped
2 T. butter
1/4 c. whipping cream

1 T. shortening
1 c. white chocolate chips
Optional: chopped nuts or
   colorful sprinkles

Melt baking chocolate in a heavy saucepan over low heat, stirring
constantly; remove from heat. Add butter and whipping cream; stir
until smooth. Refrigerate mixture for 10 to 15 minutes, stirring every
3 to 4 minutes, until mixture is firm enough to shape. Roll mixture
into one-inch balls; place on an aluminum foil-lined baking sheet.
Freeze balls for 30 minutes. Heat shortening and white chocolate chips
over low heat until smooth. Dip frozen truffles into white chocolate
and return to baking sheet. Sprinkle nuts or sprinkles over top if
desired. Refrigerate truffles for 10 to 15 minutes until coating is set.
Store in an airtight container. Makes one dozen.

A row of Amazing Double Chocolate Truffles looks so pretty
in a clear glass butter dish. Tie a satin ribbon around the dish,
and slip the recipe under the ribbon...they'll definitely
want to make these goodies again!

Cookies & Candy

Gingerbread House Dough

A good sturdy dough for constructing cut-out treats for any occasion.

2 c. shortening
2 c. sugar
2 c. molasses
2 T. cinnamon

2 t. ground cloves
2 t. baking soda
1 t. salt
9 to 10 c. all-purpose flour

Heat the first 3 ingredients in a 5-quart saucepan over low heat until sugar dissolves, stirring constantly. Remove from heat; stir in cinnamon, cloves, baking soda and salt. Gradually work in flour until a stiff dough forms; turn dough out onto a lightly floured surface and knead in as much remaining flour as possible while still maintaining a smooth consistency. Divide into 5 sections; wrap each in plastic wrap and attach baking instructions.

Instructions:

Keep dough refrigerated until ready to use. Roll each section of dough out on a lightly floured surface to 1/4-inch thickness; cut into desired forms or shapes. Arrange on lightly greased baking sheets; bake at 375 degrees for 10 to 14 minutes. Cool 3 to 4 minutes.; remove to wire rack to cool completely. Makes one large gingerbread house.

Any family will have a ball with Gingerbread House Dough, some stiff frosting for "glue" and an assortment of tasty decorations…yogurt-coated raisins, candy-coated chocolates, pretzels and cinnamon candies. Put it all in a mixing bowl and tie up with a kitchen towel. It's a fun gift for everyone!

From-My-Kitchen Oatmeal Cookie Mix

This classic is a great gift any time of the year.

1-1/3 c. quick-cooking oats, uncooked
1/2 c. brown sugar, packed
1/2 c. sugar
1/2 c. chopped pecans

1 c. chocolate chips
1 c. all-purpose flour
1 t. baking powder
1 t. baking soda
1/2 t. salt

Layer the first 5 ingredients in a one-quart, wide-mouth jar, firmly packing each layer before adding the next; set aside. Combine remaining ingredients in a small mixing bowl; mix well. Layer in jar; secure lid and attach instructions.

Instructions:

Place cookie mix in a large mixing bowl; toss gently. Add 1/2 cup melted butter, one beaten egg and one teaspoon vanilla extract; mix well. Shape dough into one-inch balls; arrange on lightly greased baking sheets. Bake at 350 degrees for 11 to 13 minutes; cool for 5 minutes on baking sheets and remove to wire racks to cool completely. Makes about 2-1/2 dozen.

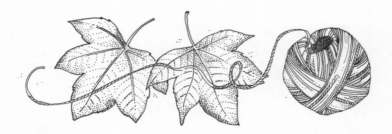

Turn a jar of From-My-Kitchen Oatmeal Cookie Mix into a beautiful fall gift...just lay a large autumn leaf over the lid, bringing the ends over the jar, and tie with jute.

1. Copy 2. Color 3. Cut Out!

Mmmm...GOOD!

(if I do say so myself)

Thanks
from
the
Heart.

It's OK to Lick the bowl... It's OK to Lick the bowl...

Cut brownies with a round cookie cutter & stack inside a glass jar.

Dip bars in chocolate, then sprinkle with nuts, jimmies or mini chips.

brownies & bars

Stack bars on vintage plates & tie up with tulle.

Use a vintage handkerchief to top jar mixes.

Include a mini cookie cutter & colored sugars for stenciling on bars.

Dark Chocolate Brownies

Sprinkle powdered sugar on top, or leave plain...either way, they're delicious.

1 c. butter, softened
6 1-oz. sqs. bittersweet baking
   chocolate
2 c. sugar
4 eggs

1 T. vanilla extract
1 c. all-purpose flour, divided
1-1/2 c. chopped walnuts
1 c. semi-sweet chocolate chips
1/4 t. salt

Melt butter and chocolate squares together in a double boiler; stir until smooth. Remove from heat; whisk in sugar, eggs and vanilla. Set aside. Toss one tablespoon flour, walnuts and chocolate chips together; stir remaining flour and salt into the sugar mixture. Fold in walnut mixture; mix well. Spread batter into a buttered 13"x9" baking pan; bake at 350 degrees for 30 to 40 minutes. Cool on a wire rack. Makes 2 dozen.

One-bite brownies! Try baking Dark Chocolate Brownies in mini muffin tins...just fill paper-lined cups with batter and reduce baking time to 25 to 35 minutes. Stack them in a metal container between colorful sheets of vellum for easy delivery.

brownies & bars

Praline Presents

*Melt butterscotch chips and pipe bows onto each square
to look like tiny gifts.*

1/2 c. shortening, melted
2 c. brown sugar, packed
2 eggs
2 t. vanilla extract

1-1/2 c. all-purpose flour
2 t. baking powder
1/2 t. salt
1 c. chopped nuts

Combine first 4 ingredients together; whisk until smooth. Mix in
remaining ingredients; spread into a buttered 13"x9" baking pan.
Bake at 350 degrees for 25 minutes; cut into squares while warm.
Makes 2 dozen.

Peanutty Polka Dots

A quick & easy treat the whole family will love.

1 lb. white melting chocolate,
   chopped
1/2 c. creamy peanut butter
2 c. crispy rice cereal

1 c. chopped peanuts
2/3 c. candy-coated chocolate
   mini-baking bits

Melt white chocolate with peanut butter over low heat in a heavy
saucepan; stir until smooth. Gradually mix in cereal and peanuts; stir
well to coat. Press mixture into a lightly buttered 13"x9" baking pan;
sprinkle candy-coated chocolates on top, pressing gently onto cereal
mixture. Set aside for 45 to 60 minutes; cut into bars to serve.
Makes 3 dozen.

Just for fun! Wrap a candy button strip around a pan of
Peanuty Polka Dots before giving to friends.

Butterscotch Bars in a Jar

Tasty enough for any occasion.

2 c. all-purpose flour
1-1/2 t. baking powder
1/4 t. salt
1/2 c. flaked coconut

1/2 c. sugar
2 c. brown sugar, packed
1/8 t. nutmeg

Combine flour, baking powder and salt together; set aside. Layer remaining ingredients in order listed in a one-quart, wide-mouth jar, pressing each layer firmly before adding the next. Add flour mixture to the top; secure lid. Attach instructions.

Instructions:

Place mix in a large mixing bowl; toss gently to mix. Add 3/4 cup softened butter, 2 beaten eggs and 2 teaspoons vanilla extract; mix until blended. Spread batter into a greased 13"x9" baking pan; bake at 375 degrees for 25 minutes. Cool. Cut into bars to serve.
Makes 2 dozen.

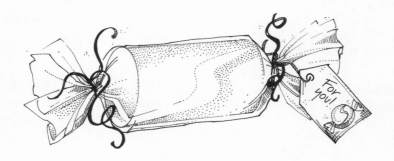

Make a big butterscotch candy! Roll Butterscotch Bars in a Jar
in several sheets of yellow cellophane, twist each end and tie
with yellow ribbons. Glue a small piece of butterscotch candy
on a gift tag and attach to the Jar...so clever!

brownies & bars

White Chocolate-Cherry Bars in a Jar

To quickly toast pecans, place them in a microwave-safe dish and heat in the microwave on high for 4 to 5 minutes, stirring after every minute.

1 c. white chocolate chips
1/2 c. chopped pecans, toasted
1/2 c. sweetened, dried cherries

1 c. brown sugar, packed and divided
2 c. buttermilk biscuit baking mix, divided

Layer the first 3 ingredients in the order listed in a one-quart, wide-mouth jar; pack down gently. Layer 1/2 cup brown sugar and one cup buttermilk biscuit mix; repeat last 2 layers. Secure lid; attach instructions.

Instructions:

Place mix in a large mixing bowl; toss gently. Add 1/2 cup butter, one egg and 2 teaspoons vanilla extract; mix well. Spread batter into a greased 9"x9" baking pan; bake at 350 degrees for 20 to 25 minutes. Cut into squares to serve. Makes 16.

The sweetest valentine! Glue a white doily to the front of White Chocolate-Cherry Bars in a Jar, then cut out a heart from red paper. Print baking instructions on the heart and glue on top of the doily.

Honey Bee Brownies

"Bee" sure to include the recipe when giving these brownies!

1-1/2 c. sugar
3/4 c. baking cocoa
3/4 c. butter, softened
3/4 c. honey

2 t. vanilla extract
4 eggs
1 c. all-purpose flour
1/2 t. salt

Combine sugar and baking cocoa in a large mixing bowl; add butter, honey and vanilla. Add eggs, one at a time, blending after each addition; gradually mix in flour and salt. Spread into a greased 13"x9" baking pan; bake at 350 degrees for 35 minutes. Cool; frost and cut into squares. Makes 2 to 3 dozen.

Chocolate Frosting:

2 c. powdered sugar
3 1-oz. sqs. bittersweet baking
    chocolate, melted

2 T. butter, melted
3 T. boiling water

Blend the first 3 ingredients together until smooth and creamy; gradually add water until desired spreading consistency is reached.

Make Honey Bee Brownie Flowers! Use a 2-inch round cookie cutter to cut out frosted brownies; stick the wide side of several pieces of candy corn around the edge and sprinkle yellow sugar in the middle. So sweet!

brownies & bars

Turtle Bars

Just like the candy, but without the fuss!

12-oz. pkg. vanilla wafers,
   finely crushed
3/4 c. butter, melted
1/8 t. salt

12-oz. pkg. semi-sweet
   chocolate chips
1 c. pecan halves
12-1/4 oz. jar caramel topping

Gently toss vanilla wafer crumbs and butter together; press into the
bottom of an ungreased 13"x9" baking pan. Sprinkle with salt,
chocolate chips and pecan halves; drizzle with caramel topping.
Bake at 350 degrees for 12 to 15 minutes; cool to room temperature.
Refrigerate until firm; cut into squares to serve. Makes 3 to 4 dozen.

Get new neighbors to come out of their shells by delivering a
batch of Turtle Bars! Take over a list of neighborhood
grocery stores, dry cleaners, doctors, dentists and hair salons.
Add a map of the town and circle popular shopping malls
and movie theaters.

Apple-Butterscotch Squares

*No one can resist the delightful combination of
apples and butterscotch.*

2 T. cornstarch
4 c. apples, cored, peeled and
   chopped
1 c. butterscotch chips
1 c. quick-cooking oats,
   uncooked

18-1/2 oz. pkg. yellow cake mix
3/4 c. butter, softened
1 t. cinnamon
1/2 c. brown sugar, packed
1/4 c. wheat germ

Combine first 3 ingredients in a large saucepan; heat until chips have
melted. Set aside. Mix oats, cake mix and butter together until coarse
crumbs form; set one cup mixture aside and press remaining crumbs
into an ungreased 13"x9" baking pan. Spread apple mixture on top;
sprinkle with cinnamon. Combine reserved crumb mixture with brown
sugar and wheat germ; layer over apple mixture. Bake at 350 degrees
for 35 to 45 minutes; cool at least 30 minutes. Cut into squares.
Makes about 2 dozen.

Crafty friends will love receiving a knitting gift basket.
Pick out colorful yarn, needles in different sizes and
an easy-to-make pattern. Pack all the materials in a handy
tote that can be used for future projects. Don't forget to tuck
in some sweets to snack on while stitching!

brownies & bars

Calico Fruit Treats

A colorful dessert that's great for potlucks or carry-ins.

2 c. all-purpose flour
2 c. sugar
1 t. baking soda
1 t. cinnamon
1/2 t. salt
1 c. oil

2 t. vanilla extract
2 c. bananas, diced
1 c. maraschino cherries, halved
3 eggs, beaten
8-oz. can crushed pineapple

Combine all ingredients; mix well. Spread into a greased and floured jelly-roll pan; bake at 350 degrees for 30 to 40 minutes or until a toothpick inserted in the center removes clean. Drizzle with glaze; cool and cut into bars to serve. Cover and store in the refrigerator. Makes 4 dozen.

Glaze:

1/4 c. butter, softened
1-3/4 c. powdered sugar

1 to 2 T. warm water

Whisk ingredients together until smooth and creamy.

to:

from:

Malt Chocolate Brownies

Your friends will think you baked all day.

12-oz. pkg. milk chocolate chips
1/2 c. butter, softened
3/4 c. sugar
1 t. vanilla extract
3 eggs

1-3/4 c. all-purpose flour
1/2 c. malted milk powder
1/2 t. salt
1 c. malted milk balls, coarsely
    chopped

Melt chocolate chips and butter in a 3-quart saucepan over low heat, stirring frequently; remove from heat. Set aside to cool slightly; blend in sugar, vanilla and eggs. Add flour, malted milk powder and salt; spread batter in a greased 13"x9" baking pan. Sprinkle with malted milk balls; bake at 350 degrees for 30 to 35 minutes. Cool. Cut into bars to serve. Makes 2 dozen.

Pair Malt Chocolate Brownies with a set of old-fashioned malt glasses before delivering to friends. Add some sprinkles, whipped topping, a jar of maraschino cherries and gift tag with instructions: "Add vanilla ice cream to make a marvelous Malt Chocolate Brownie Sundae."

Fudge Nut Bites

Just as delicious with pecans, peanuts or cashews.

1 c. butter, softened
2 c. brown sugar, packed
2 eggs
1-1/2 t. vanilla extract

3 c. quick-cooking oats,
    uncooked
2 c. all-purpose flour
1 t. baking soda
1 t. salt

Cream butter and sugar in a large mixing bowl; add eggs and vanilla, mixing well. Set aside. Combine remaining ingredients; gradually blend into sugar mixture. Spread 3/4 of the dough into an ungreased 17"x11" rimmed baking pan; spread filling on top. Set aside. Roll remaining dough out very thin between 2 sheets wax paper; cut into desired shapes using mini cookie cutters. Arrange on top of filling; bake at 350 degrees for 25 to 30 minutes. Cool for 10 minutes; cut into squares while still warm. Cool; store in an airtight container. Makes 3-1/2 dozen.

Filling:

7-oz. can sweetened condensed
    milk
1 c. milk chocolate chips

1 T. butter
1/2 t. salt
1/2 c. chopped walnuts

Combine milk, chocolate chips and butter in a heavy saucepan; heat over low heat until chips melt. Whisk in salt until smooth and creamy; stir in walnuts.

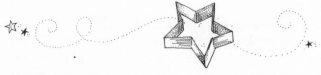

Use a mini star cookie cutter to cut out shapes from the top crust of Fudge Nut Bites. Arrange them on top of the filling, so when cut, each square will have a star.

Extra Chocolate Chip Bars in a Jar

Triple chocolate chips in every bite!

1/4 c. milk chocolate chips
1/4 c. white chocolate chips
1/4 c. semi-sweet chocolate
   chips
1/2 c. chopped walnuts, toasted
   and cooled

1/2 c. dark brown sugar, packed
2 c. buttermilk biscuit baking
   mix, divided
1/2 c. light brown sugar, packed

Layer and gently pack first 5 ingredients in a one-quart,
wide-mouth jar; add one cup buttermilk biscuit baking mix, light
brown sugar and remaining buttermilk biscuit baking mix. Secure
lid; attach instructions.

Instructions:

Place mix in a large mixing bowl; toss gently. Blend in 1/2 cup
softened butter, one egg and 2 teaspoons vanilla extract; press
mixture into a lightly greased 8"x8" baking pan. Bake at 350 degrees
until golden, about 25 to 30 minutes. Cool; cut into bars. Makes 16.

A chocolate lover's dream! Fill an old-fashioned scoop
with wrapped milk chocolate and white chocolate drops.
Wrap the scoop in cellophane and tie a ribbon around
the handle to secure. Deliver with Extra Chocolate Chip Bars
in a Jar...add a note that says, "A scoop of hugs & kisses
and sweet wishes for you!"

brownies & bars

Cookie Bars in a Jar

Give with a can of sweetened condensed milk...friends will only need to add butter to make these scrumptious bars.

1/2 c. chopped nuts
1 c. butterscotch chips
1 c. chocolate chips

1 c. flaked coconut
1/2 t. salt
1-1/2 c. graham cracker crumbs

Layer ingredients in the order listed in a one-quart, wide-mouth jar. Secure lid; attach instructions.

Instructions:

Spoon graham cracker crumbs into a small mixing bowl; toss with 1/2 cup melted butter. Pat into the bottom of an ungreased 11"x7" baking pan; sprinkle remaining mix on top. Pour a 14-ounce can sweetened condensed milk over the top; bake at 350 degrees for 30 minutes. Cool; cut into bars to serve. Makes 3 dozen.

Create a clever tote for jar mixes. Before screwing on the lid, lay the middle of a length of ribbon across the top of the jar, so the ends trail down the sides. Secure the lid tightly, then bring the ribbon ends up and tie in a bow to make a handle.

Walnut-Raspberry Brownies

Try topping with different jams like strawberry, grape or peach.

3 1-oz. sqs. unsweetened
   baking chocolate
1/2 c. shortening
3 eggs
1-1/2 c. sugar

2 t. vanilla extract
1/2 t. salt
1 c. all-purpose flour
1-1/2 c. chopped walnuts
1/3 c. raspberry jam

Melt chocolate squares with shortening in a double boiler; cool slightly.
Blend eggs, sugar, vanilla and salt together in large mixing bowl; add
melted chocolate mixture and flour, mixing well. Fold in walnuts;
spread into a greased 8"x8" baking pan. Bake at 325 degrees for
40 minutes; spread jam over hot brownies. Set aside to cool
completely; cut into squares to serve. Makes 16.

Friendship Day is the first Sunday in August. Celebrate by
filling an old-fashioned milk carrier with 2 bottles of milk and
2 stacks of Walnut-Raspberry Brownies...tuck in some napkins
and surprise a friend with a yummy afternoon treat.

brownies & bars

Double Cherry Crumb Bars

The best of a brownie and cobbler in one tasty recipe.

2 c. water
1 c. dried cherries, chopped
2 c. quick-cooking oats,
  uncooked
1-1/2 c. all-purpose flour
1-1/2 c. brown sugar, packed

1 t. baking powder
1/2 t. baking soda
1 c. butter
2 c. cherry preserves
1/2 c. slivered almonds

Bring water to a boil in a saucepan; remove from heat. Add cherries; let stand for 10 minutes. Drain fruit and set aside. Combine oats, flour, brown sugar, baking powder and baking soda together; cut in butter with a pastry cutter until coarse crumbs form. Reserve one cup crumb mixture; press remaining crumbs into the bottom of an ungreased jelly-roll pan. Bake at 350 degrees for 12 minutes; set aside. Stir cherries and cherry preserves together; spread over crust. Toss almonds with reserved crumb mixture; sprinkle over cherry mixture. Bake 20 to 25 minutes until top is golden; cool completely before cutting into bars. Makes 4 dozen.

Give a pan of Double Cherry Crumb Bars with a stack of ice cream bowls, colorful plastic spoons and several half-pint containers of ice cream. Yum!

Oh-So-Special Brownies in a Jar

An easy and memorable gift for those sweet occasions.

1 c. all-purpose flour
1 t. baking soda
1 t. salt
1/2 t. vanilla powder
2/3 c. brown sugar, packed
1/3 c. baking cocoa

1 c. white chocolate chips
1 c. semi-sweet chocolate chips
1/2 c. chopped nuts
2/3 c. sugar

Combine first 4 ingredients; press into a one-quart, wide-mouth jar. Layer remaining ingredients in order listed, packing each layer gently before adding the next. Secure lid; attach instructions.

Instructions:

Place mix in a large mixing bowl; toss gently. Add 3 eggs and 2/3 cup oil; mix well. Spread into a greased 9"x9" baking pan; bake at 350 degrees for 35 to 40 minutes. Cool. Cut into squares to serve. Makes 15 to 18.

Tuck Oh-So-Special Brownies in a Jar inside a heart-shaped pan and wrap a fluffy square of tulle around it all. Be sure to add a heart or kiss-shaped gift tag with baking instructions...a great gift for Valentine's Day or anniversaries.

brownies & bars

Nutty Butterscotch Bars in a Jar

An old favorite or a new tradition…these are sure to please.

1 c. butterscotch chips
1/2 c. pecan pieces, toasted and
   cooled
1/2 c. light brown sugar, packed

2 c. buttermilk biscuit baking
   mix, divided
1/2 c. dark brown sugar, packed

Gently layer and pack the first 3 ingredients in a one-quart, wide-mouth jar; layer one cup buttermilk biscuit baking mix, dark brown sugar and remaining buttermilk baking mix. Secure lid; attach instructions.

Instructions:

Place mix in a medium mixing bowl; toss gently. Stir in 1/2 cup melted butter, one egg and 2 teaspoons vanilla extract; mix well. Press into a greased 8"x8" baking pan; bake at 350 degrees for 18 to 20 minutes. Cool; slice into bars to serve. Makes 15 to 18.

Great for the lazy days of Summer. Deliver Nutty Butterscotch Bars in a Jar with a good book and slip a homemade bookmark inside. Just cut out a bookmark from cardstock, glue a strip of decorative paper on top and decorate with stickers.

Full of Peanuts Bars

A chewy brownie rolled in nuts.

1-1/2 c. all-purpose flour	2 T. butter
1-1/2 t. baking powder	1 c. sugar
1/2 t. salt	1 egg
1/2 c. milk	3 c. chopped peanuts

Combine first 3 ingredients; set aside. Heat milk and butter in small saucepan; stir until butter melts. Set aside to cool slightly. Blend sugar and egg together in a medium mixing bowl; mix in milk mixture. Gradually add flour mixture; stir until just combined. Spread in a greased and floured 13"x9" baking pan; bake at 325 degrees for 20 to 24 minutes. Cool to room temperature; cut into 24 bars. Frost tops and sides with Butter Cream Frosting; roll in chopped peanuts. Frost bottoms; roll in chopped peanuts. Makes 2 dozen.

Butter Cream Frosting:

1/2 c. butter, softened	4 c. powdered sugar
1 t. vanilla extract	1/4 c. milk

Blend butter and vanilla until light and fluffy; gradually add powdered sugar alternately with milk. Add additional milk, if necessary, until desired spreading consistency is reached.

Fun for the whole family! Deliver a batch of
Full of Peanuts Bars with tickets to the circus.

brownies & bars

Peanut Butter Kiss Bars

*Try topping squares with different kinds of
bite-size candies...a sweet surprise every time!*

1/2 c. creamy peanut butter
1/4 c. butter, softened
1 c. brown sugar, packed
2 eggs

1 t. almond extract
2/3 c. all-purpose flour
1 c. chopped peanuts, divided
16 milk chocolate drops

Cream first 3 ingredients together until light and fluffy; blend in
eggs and almond extract. Add flour and 3/4 cup chopped peanuts; mix
well. Spread in a greased 9"x9" baking pan; sprinkle with remaining
peanuts. Bake at 350 degrees for 25 to 30 minutes; remove from oven
and immediately press milk chocolate drops evenly over the top,
allowing for space to cut into squares. Cool completely. Cut into
squares to serve. Makes 16.

Marshmallow 4-Layer Goodies

*Substitute candy-coated chocolates, chopped peanuts and raisins in
place of the chocolate chips, pecans and coconut
for a whole new flavor.*

18-1/2 oz. pkg. yellow cake mix
1/4 c. margarine, melted
1/4 c. water
3 c. mini marshmallows

1 c. chocolate chips
1/4 c. chopped pecans
1/2 c. flaked coconut

Combine first 3 ingredients; press into a greased 13"x9" baking pan.
Bake at 375 degrees for 20 minutes; remove from oven. Layer
remaining ingredients on top; bake until marshmallows begin to melt,
about 2 to 3 minutes. Cool; cut into bars. Makes 2 dozen.

Apple-Oat Cinnamon Squares

Have a cold glass of milk handy when giving these yummy snacks.

3 c. biscuit baking mix
2 c. quick-cooking oats,
   uncooked
2/3 c. plus 2 T. brown sugar,
   packed and divided

1 t. cinnamon
1/2 c. butter, sliced
1 c. milk
21-oz. can apple pie filling

Combine biscuit baking mix, oats, 2/3 cup brown sugar and cinnamon together; cut in butter with a pastry cutter until coarse crumbs form. Stir in milk until just moistened; fold in apple pie filling. Spread in a lightly greased 13"x9" baking pan; sprinkle with remaining brown sugar. Bake at 350 degrees for 40 minutes; cool. Cut into squares to serve. Makes 16.

Stack 2 to 3 Apple-Oat Cinnamon Squares on top of mini chalk boards. Wrap each with cellophane, tie with a bow and tuck in some pencils or a box of chalk...great for teachers and school staff.

brownies & bars

Quick Crescent Jam Sweets

Make several batches of these easy bars...use a different jam in each.

8-oz. tube refrigerated crescent
   rolls
1/2 to 3/4 c. strawberry jam
1/3 c. sugar
1/3 c. all-purpose flour

1/2 t. cinnamon
1/4 t. nutmeg
1/4 c. butter
Garnish: powdered sugar

Separate crescent roll dough into 4 rectangles; press 2 rectangles into
the bottom and 1/4 inch up the sides of an ungreased 8"x8" baking
pan, pinching seams to seal. Spread jam on top; arrange remaining
2 dough rectangles on top, gently stretching to cover jam. Set aside.
Combine remaining ingredients; sprinkle over dough. Bake at
375 degrees for 20 to 25 minutes; cool and cut into bars. Sprinkle with
powdered sugar before serving. Makes 18 servings.

Apple-Cheddar Breakfast Bars

*Take a basket of these to the bus stop to share with kids on the
first day of school.*

1 c. brown sugar, packed
2 eggs
3 c. apples, cored, peeled and
   chopped
1 c. all-purpose flour

2 t. baking powder
1 t. salt
1 c. shredded Cheddar cheese
3/4 c. chopped nuts
1/4 c. flaked coconut

Combine sugar and eggs; mix well. Fold in apples; add remaining
ingredients. Spread into a greased and floured 13"x9" baking pan;
bake at 375 degrees for 20 to 25 minutes. Cool; cut into bars. Makes
2 to 3 dozen.

Dutch Almond Bars

*For a sweeter version, mix together one cup powdered sugar,
one tablespoon milk and 1/4 teaspoon vanilla extract...drizzle
over warm bars.*

1 c. butter
3/4 c. sugar
1 egg yolk
2 c. all-purpose flour

1-1/2 t. cinnamon
1/4 t. baking soda
1 egg white, beaten
1/2 c. sliced almonds

Cream butter for 30 seconds; blend in sugar until light and fluffy. Mix
in egg yolk; set aside. Combine flour, cinnamon and baking soda; add
to butter mixture, stirring until just combined. Press dough evenly
into the bottom of an ungreased jelly-roll pan; brush with egg white.
Sprinkle with almonds, pressing lightly into dough. Bake at
350 degrees for 15 to 18 minutes; let cool for 5 minutes. Cut into
squares; remove to a wire rack to cool completely. Makes 3 dozen.

Keep in touch with faraway friends and encourage them to do
the same by sending them a box of stationery, postage
stamps and a pen. Be sure to include some homemade treats
that travel well like Dutch Almond Bars!

brownies & bars

Mocha Banana Bars

No one will guess how easy these are!

18-1/2 oz. pkg. yellow cake mix
1-1/4 c. banana, thinly sliced
1 c. buttermilk
1/4 c. cold coffee
2 eggs

Blend ingredients together; pour into a greased jelly-roll pan. Bake at 350 degrees for 25 to 35 minutes or until a toothpick inserted in the center removes clean; set aside to cool. Frost with Mocha Frosting; cut into bars to serve. Makes 3 dozen.

Mocha Frosting:

1-1/3 c. powdered sugar
1/2 t. salt
1 T. butter
2 to 3 T. cold coffee

Whisk ingredients together until smooth and creamy.

Take a basket of Mocha Banana Bars to work and place one on each co-worker's desk with a package of instant cappuccino...a great Monday morning pick-me-up!

Frosted Peanut Butter Brownies

The ultimate ooey-gooey treat!

1-1/2 c. butter, divided
2/3 c. baking cocoa, divided
2 c. sugar
1-1/2 c. all-purpose flour
1 t. salt
4 eggs

1 t. vanilla extract
18-oz. jar crunchy peanut butter
10 marshmallows
1/3 c. milk
1-lb. pkg. powdered sugar

Heat one cup butter and 1/3 cup baking cocoa in a saucepan over low heat until butter melts; stir often. Remove from heat; set aside to cool slightly. Combine sugar, flour and salt in a large mixing bowl; blend in chocolate mixture. Add eggs and vanilla; spread in a greased jelly-roll pan. Bake at 350 degrees for 20 minutes or until a toothpick inserted in the center removes clean. Melt peanut butter; spread over warm brownies. Chill for 30 minutes. Melt marshmallows and remaining butter with milk in a heavy saucepan over low heat, stirring often; remove from heat. Whisk in remaining cocoa; gradually stir in powdered sugar until smooth and creamy. Spread over peanut butter layer; refrigerate until firm, at least 20 minutes. Cut into squares to serve. Makes 6 dozen.

Bite-size goodies are easy to tote and so much fun for sampling! Cut Frosted Peanut Butter Brownies into one-inch squares and place each inside a paper candy cup...line them up in a basket and take to the next potluck, church social or school party.

brownies & bars

Creamy Peppermint Brownies

Delight friends with chocolate and mint in a terrific brownie!

1-1/2 c. butter, melted
3 c. sugar
1-1/2 T. vanilla extract
5 eggs
2 c. all-purpose flour

1 c. baking cocoa
1 t. baking powder
1 t. salt
24 chocolate-covered
   mint patties

Cream butter and sugar; blend in vanilla and eggs. Add flour,
cocoa, baking powder and salt; mix well. Set 2 cups batter to the
side; spread remaining batter in an ungreased 13"x9" baking pan.
Arrange mint patties in a single layer about 1/2 inch apart on top
of the batter; spread with reserved batter. Bake at 350 degrees for
50 to 55 minutes; cool completely before cutting into squares.
Makes 3 dozen.

diamonds are a girl's best friend

A girl's best friend! Slice a pan of Creamy Peppermint
Brownies diagonally to create diamonds, then cut extra
chocolate-covered mint patties into quarters and stick one in
each diamond, so the cream shows...it adds a sparkle.

Just Peachie Bars

Try orange marmalade or strawberry preserves too.

8-oz. tube refrigerated crescent
    rolls
8-oz. pkg. cream cheese,
    softened
1/4 c. sugar

3 T. all-purpose flour
1 T. lemon juice
1 egg
1/2 c. peach preserves
1/3 c. flaked coconut, toasted

Separate crescent roll dough into 2 rectangles; press into the bottom and 1/2 inch up the sides of an ungreased 13"x9" baking pan, pinching seams to seal. Set aside. Blend cream cheese and sugar until light and fluffy; stir in flour, lemon juice and egg; spread over crust. Bake at 375 degrees for 18 to 22 minutes; spread with preserves and sprinkle with coconut. Refrigerate until chilled. Makes 2 dozen.

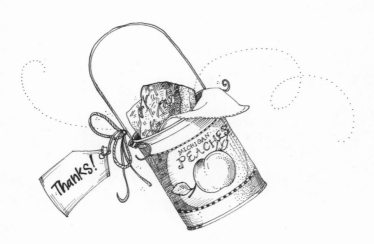

A vintage tin can makes a classic tote for Just Peachie Bars. Punch 2 holes near the rim of the can and thread the ends of a wire through each, rounding the ends to secure the handle. Line the inside with a cheery kitchen towel and fill!

brownies & bars

Snowy Lemon Bars

No need to wait for a special occasion...whip up these bars
for a good friend, just because.

3 eggs, divided
1/3 c. butter, melted
1 T. lemon zest
3 T. lemon juice
18-1/2 oz. pkg. white cake mix
1 c. chopped almonds

8-oz. pkg. cream cheese,
  softened
3 c. powdered sugar
Garnish: additional powdered
  sugar

Combine one egg, butter, lemon zest and lemon juice; add cake mix
and almonds, mixing well. Press into the bottom of a greased
13"x9" baking pan; bake at 350 degrees until golden, about
15 minutes. Set aside. Blend cream cheese until light and fluffy;
gradually mix in powdered sugar. Add remaining eggs, one at a time,
blending well after each addition; pour over hot crust. Bake for 15 to
20 minutes longer or until center is set; cool on a wire rack. Garnish
with powdered sugar before cutting into bars to serve. Makes 2 dozen.

Pipe meringue in snowflake patterns on top of
Snowy Lemon Bars for an extra-special garnish
before taking to the holiday party hostess.

Chocolatey Caramel Delights

These little treats will be a big hit!

1 c. all-purpose flour   1/3 c. sugar
1/2 c. butter, softened

Combine ingredients until coarse crumbs form; press into an ungreased 9"x9" baking pan; bake at 350 degrees for 15 to 20 minutes. Spread with filling; bake for 15 to 20 additional minutes. Cut into small squares while warm; cool completely on wire racks. Makes 3 dozen.

Filling:

2 eggs   1/2 t. vanilla extract
1/2 c. sugar   1/4 t. salt
1/2 c. corn syrup   1/2 c. flaked coconut
1/4 c. crunchy peanut butter   1/2 c. milk chocolate chips

Blend eggs and sugar together; add corn syrup, peanut butter, vanilla and salt. Fold in coconut and chocolate chips; stir gently.

Nestle squares of Chocolatey Caramel Delights inside an oversized mug and tuck in a packet of cocoa...an early morning surprise for co-workers or neighbors.

brownies & bars

Gingerbread Brownie Mix

Lots of sweet with just enough spice.

1-1/2 c. all-purpose flour	1 t. cinnamon
1 c. sugar	1/2 t. baking soda
1/4 c. baking cocoa	1/2 t. ground cloves
1 t. allspice	

Combine ingredients in a large mixing bowl; spoon into a plastic zipping bag. Attach instructions.

Instructions:

Place mix in a medium mixing bowl; toss gently. Blend in 1/4 cup melted butter, 1/3 cup molasses and 2 eggs. Spread into a greased 13"x9" baking pan; bake at 350 degrees for 20 minutes. Cool on a wire rack; cut into bars. Makes 2 dozen.

Make scented gift tags for Gingerbread Brownie Mix.
Glue a sheet of sandpaper to brown colored paper. Use a cookie cutter to trace a gingerbread man design on the paper and cut it out. Scent with spices by rubbing a cinnamon stick over the sandpaper. Paint on eyes, a nose, buttons and a mouth...print the baking instructions on the back.

#1 Buckeye Bars

Tastes just like the mouth-watering candy, but made in a pan.

1 c. butter
1-1/2 c. creamy peanut butter, divided

1-lb. pkg. powdered sugar
8-oz. milk chocolate candy bar

Place butter, one cup peanut butter and powdered sugar in a heavy saucepan; heat over low heat until creamy and smooth, stirring often. Spread into an ungreased 13"x9" baking pan; set aside to cool to room temperature. Melt chocolate bar and remaining peanut butter together in a small saucepan over low heat; stir constantly. Pour over peanut butter-sugar layer; refrigerate until firm. Cut into bars to serve. Makes 2 to 3 dozen.

Surprise tailgaters with a spirited treat! Arrange Number One Buckeye Bars in the shape of a "1" on a serving platter and write "Go Team" in melted chocolate around the edges of the platter.

brownies & bars

Banana Chip Brownies

Chocolate and bananas...a yummy combination kids love.

10-oz. pkg. brownie mix
1 c. quick-cooking oats,
   uncooked
1 egg
3 to 4 T. water

1 c. dried banana chips, coarsely
   chopped
1 c. milk chocolate chips
1 c. mini marshmallows
3/4 c. chopped peanuts

Combine brownie mix, oats, egg and water in medium mixing bowl;
spread evenly in a greased 13"x9" baking pan. Bake at 325 degrees
for 5 minutes. Sprinkle with remaining ingredients, pressing
ingredients down gently with the back of a spoon. Bake for
15 additional minutes; cool in pan on a wire rack. Cut into bars to
serve. Makes 2 dozen.

Slip Banana Chip Brownies inside vellum envelopes and
tie them closed with shoestring licorice...fun for kids
of all ages!

Old-Time Oatmeal Bars

Creamy chocolate between layers of chewy oats.

1-1/2 c. plus 2 T. butter,
   softened and divided
1 c. semi-sweet chocolate chips
2/3 c. evaporated milk
1/3 c. sugar
1 c. brown sugar, packed

1 egg
1 t. vanilla extract
1-1/4 c. all-purpose flour
1/2 t. baking soda
2 c. quick-cooking oats,
   uncooked and divided

Melt 2 tablespoons butter with chocolate chips in a heavy saucepan;
add evaporated milk and sugar. Bring to a rolling boil, stirring
constantly; remove from heat and set aside to cool. Cream remaining
butter with brown sugar; add egg and vanilla, blending until light
and fluffy. Mix in flour, baking soda and 1-3/4 cups oats; press
2/3 mixture into the bottom of a greased 9"x9" baking pan. Spread
chocolate mixture on top; set aside. Toss remaining oats with
remaining crumb mixture; sprinkle on top of chocolate layer. Bake at
350 degrees for 25 to 30 minutes. Cool and slice into bars to serve.
Makes 3 dozen.

A charming gift for anyone! Arrange squares of
Old-Time Oatmeal Bars on a mini cutting board. Wrap clear
plastic wrap around them to keep extra fresh, and tie a big
checkered ribbon around the handle.

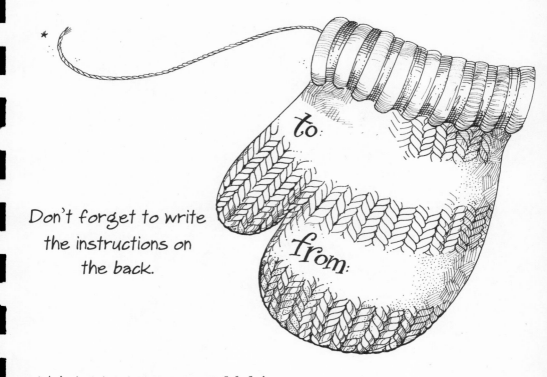

to:

from:

Don't forget to write
the instructions on
the back.

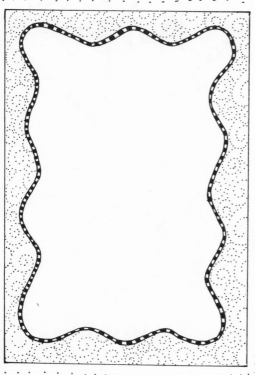

"Life
itself
is the proper
binge."

- Julia Child -

Make a copy of these little tags & tie them on for extra·special gifts.

Eat dessert first!

from the Kitchen of:

be happy

Tie a new ice cream scoop onto a jar of hot fudge sauce.

Hot Fudge Sauce

For You!

Set mini cupcakes inside a vintage cake mold.

Cakes, Pies, & More

Pie Crust Mix

Include a pie bird with your pie crust mix.

oh happy day!

Line peppermints or butterscotch candies around the border of a pie.

Give a cake with plastic forks, paper plates & napkins...no clean-up!

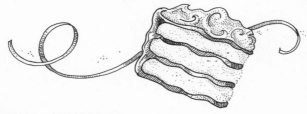

Apple Crisp Gift Kit

Give these to your busiest friends...they don't even have to add additional ingredients!

2 c. all-purpose flour
1 c. brown sugar, packed
1 c. long-cooking oats, uncooked
1 t. cinnamon

1/2 t. salt
1/4 t. nutmeg
1 c. chilled butter
1 c. chopped pecans
4 21-oz. cans apple pie filling

Combine first 6 ingredients in a large mixing bowl; cut in butter with a pastry cutter until coarse crumbs form. Gently toss in pecans. Divide mixture into 2 plastic zipping bags; store in the refrigerator. Give each bag of topping with 2 cans of apple pie filling; attach instructions. Prepare within 6 weeks. Makes 2 kits.

Instructions:

Spread 2 cans apple pie filling in a lightly buttered 13"x9" baking pan; sprinkle topping over apples. Bake at 400 degrees until topping is golden and apples are bubbly, about 18 to 20 minutes. Serve warm. Makes 12 servings.

Attach a bag of caramels to an Apple Crisp Gift Kit...friends can stir them in before baking or melt and drizzle over top of a baked crisp.

cakes, pies & more!

Homecoming Cobbler Mix

Be sure to present with a basket brimming with at least 4 cups fresh berries...strawberries, blueberries or raspberries make delicious cobblers.

1 c. all-purpose flour	1 t. vanilla powder
1 t. baking powder	4 c. fresh berries
1 c. sugar	

Combine first 4 ingredients; spoon into a plastic zipping bag. Place berries in a basket; attach instructions.

Instructions:

Combine berries, 1/4 cup orange juice, 1/4 cup sugar and one teaspoon cinnamon; spread in an ungreased 13"x9" baking pan. In a medium mixing bowl, whisk one cup melted butter and one egg together; stir in cobbler mix. Drop by tablespoonfuls onto fruit mixture; bake at 375 degrees for 35 to 45 minutes. Cool for 15 minutes before serving. Makes 8 to 10 servings.

Place Homecoming Cobbler Mix inside a new mailbox and deliver to friends in a brand new home...tuck in some address stickers for the mailbox too!

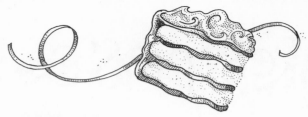

1-2-3 Cheesecake

Mix, bake and refrigerate!

2 8-oz. pkgs. cream cheese,
   softened
1/2 c. sugar
1 t. vanilla extract

2 eggs
1/2 c. mini semi-sweet chocolate
   chips
9-inch graham cracker pie crust

Blend cream cheese, sugar and vanilla until light and fluffy; mix
in eggs. Fold in chocolate chips; spread into pie crust. Bake at
350 degrees for 40 minutes or until center is almost set; cool to room
temperature. Refrigerate for at least 3 hours before serving. Makes
8 servings.

Jazz up 1-2-3 Cheesecake by adding chocolate stars on top.
Just melt one cup chocolate chips with one tablespoon
shortening; pour it in a jelly-roll pan lined with foil and
refrigerate just until firm. Lightly grease star-shaped
cookie cutters and cut out chocolate stars. Stand them
in the cake so they're upright...so easy!

cakes, pies & more!

Sunny Lemon Cake

A pretty cake that holds its shape when baked in a fluted pan.

1-1/2 c. butter, softened
3 c. sugar
5 eggs
3 c. all-purpose flour

3/4 c. lemon-lime soda
2 T. lemon extract
1 t. lemon zest

Cream butter and sugar until light and fluffy; add eggs, one at a time, blending well after each addition. Mix in flour, one cup at a time; add lemon-lime soda, lemon extract and lemon zest, mixing well. Pour into a greased and floured 10" tube pan; bake at 350 degrees for 60 to 65 minutes or until a toothpick inserted in the center removes clean. Cool on wire rack in pan for 10 minutes; loosen sides of cake and remove from pan. Cool. Makes 12 servings.

Share a burst of sunshine with everyone at the next Memorial Day picnic. Divide Sunny Lemon Cake batter between several mini Bundt® pans to make smaller cakes. When cooled, invert them onto round doilies and wrap up with cellophane...top each off with a big yellow bow.

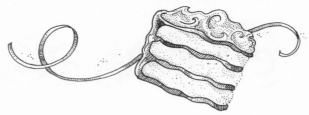

Amazin' Raisin Cake

This is the cake to give when celebrating a job well-done!

3 c. all-purpose flour
2 c. sugar
1 c. mayonnaise
1/3 c. milk
2 eggs
2 t. baking soda
2 t. cinnamon

1/2 t. nutmeg
1/2 t. salt
1/4 t. ground cloves
3 c. apples, cored, peeled and
   chopped
1 c. raisins

Combine the first 10 ingredients together; blend on low speed of an electric mixer for 2 minutes. Fold in apples and raisins; spread batter into 2 greased and floured 9" round baking pans. Bake at 350 degrees for 45 minutes or until a toothpick inserted in the center removes clean; set aside to cool for 10 minutes. Remove cakes from pans; cool completely on wire racks. Place one layer on a serving plate; frost sides and top. Place second layer on top; frost completely. Makes 8 to 10 servings.

Frosting:

2 c. whipping cream

1/2 c. powdered sugar

Whisk or blend ingredients together until stiff peaks form.

Plum Delicious Cake

Plum perfection in every bite!

1/4 c. butter, softened	1 T. orange zest
1/2 c. sugar	3/4 t. baking powder
2 eggs	1/2 t. nutmeg
3 T. orange juice	1-lb. pkg. plums, quartered
1 c. all-purpose flour	

Cream butter and sugar in a large mixing bowl until light and fluffy; add eggs and orange juice. Set aside. Combine flour, zest, baking powder and nutmeg; gradually blend into sugar mixture. Spread in a buttered parchment paper-lined 10" springform pan; gently arrange plum quarters on top, skin-side up. Spread with filling; sprinkle with streusel. Bake at 350 degrees for 60 to 70 minutes or until a toothpick inserted in the center remove clean; cool. Remove from pan. Makes 8 to 10 servings.

Filling:

1-1/4 c. sour cream	2 T. orange juice
1 egg	1 t. cornstarch

Blend until smooth and creamy.

Streusel:

1 c. all-purpose flour	1/2 t. cinnamon
1/2 c. brown sugar, packed	1/2 c. butter
1/2 t. nutmeg	

Combine first 4 ingredients; cut in butter using a pastry cutter until mixture resembles coarse crumbs.

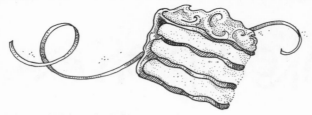

Picnic Carrot Cake Mix

Give with a container of cream cheese frosting...delicious!

2 c. sugar
2 t. vanilla powder
1/2 c. chopped pecans
3 c. all-purpose flour

2 t. baking soda
1 T. cinnamon
1/4 t. nutmeg
1/8 t. ground cloves

Combine ingredients together; place in a plastic zipping bag. Attach instructions.

Instructions:

Place Carrot Cake Mix in a large mixing bowl; form a well in the center. Add 1-1/2 cup oil, 3 eggs, 3 cups grated carrots and an 8-ounce can crushed pineapple; mix well. Pour into a greased 13"x9" baking pan; bake at 350 degrees for 40 to 50 minutes or until a toothpick inserted in the center removes clean. Cool. Makes 18 servings.

A quick springtime gift. Gather a bunch of carrots, a can of pineapple and Picnic Carrot Cake Mix...tuck inside a big picnic basket filled with Easter grass.

cakes, pies & more!

Easiest Pumpkin Cupcakes

Short on time? Whip up these cupcakes in the blink of an eye using a spice cake mix.

18-1/4 oz. pkg. spice cake mix
15-oz. can pumpkin
3 eggs
1/3 c. oil

1/3 c. water
16-oz. container cream cheese
   frosting

Stir together cake mix, pumpkin, eggs, oil and water in a large bowl until well blended. Beat with an electric mixture on medium speed for 2 minutes. Pour batter into greased muffin cups, filling each 3/4 full. Bake at 350 degrees for 18 to 22 minutes or until centers test done. Cool in pans for 10 minutes; place cupcakes on wire racks to cool completely. Spread frosting over each. Makes 2 dozen.

Dip mini cookie cutters into cinnamon, then lightly press the image into the frosted tops of Easiest Pumpkin Cupcakes...the cinnamon will stay on the cupcake in the cookie-cutter design. Mini pumpkins and fall leaves are sweet shapes to try.

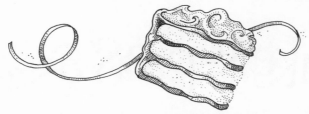

Family-Style Chocolate Pudding Mix

For a mocha flavor, add one teaspoon instant coffee granules to the mix.

2-1/2 c. powdered milk
3 c. cornstarch
5 c. sugar

1-1/2 c. baking cocoa
1-1/2 t. salt

Combine ingredients together; store in an airtight container. Attach instructions. Makes 12 cups.

Instructions:

Shake mix before using; measure out 2/3 cup mix and place in a saucepan. Add 2 cups milk; heat over low heat. Stir until mixture thickens and boils; continue stirring for one minute. Remove from heat; pour into individual serving dishes. Refrigerate until chilled. Makes 10 servings.

Giving a pudding mix in the summer? Pair the mix with some paper cups and popsicle sticks to make pudding pops. Just add an extra line to the instructions: "Spoon cooled pudding into paper cups and insert a popsicle stick in the centers; freeze 3 to 4 hours, then peel off the paper cups."

Favorite Vanilla Pudding Mix

Want to switch it up? Leave out the nutmeg and substitute any extract in place of vanilla when cooking...lemon, banana and pineapple are all delicious!

1-1/4 c. powdered milk	1/2 t. salt
1-1/2 c. sugar	1-1/4 c. cornstarch
1/4 t. nutmeg	1/2 t. vanilla powder

Mix all ingredients together; store in an airtight container. Attach a gift tag with instructions. Makes 3 cups.

Instructions:

Mix 1/2 cup mix with 2 cups milk in a saucepan. Stirring constantly, bring mixture to a boil; reduce heat and simmer until thickened, stirring constantly. Remove from heat. Pour pudding into individual serving dishes; refrigerate until chilled. Serves 4 to 6.

Oversized craft punches turn out great gift tags! Look for circles, squares, ovals and triangles at the local craft store and use them to cut out perfect shapes from colored paper. Stamp designs on the front and write a greeting on the back.

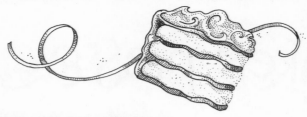

Praline Ice Cream Syrup

*Use dark corn syrup and dark brown sugar for a
richer color and flavor.*

2 c. corn syrup
1/3 c. brown sugar, packed
1/2 c. water
1-1/4 c. chopped pecans

1/2 t. vanilla extract
4 1-pint canning jars and lids,
   sterilized

Combine syrup, sugar and water in a saucepan; heat over medium
heat and bring to a boil. Boil for one minute; remove from heat. Stir in
pecans and vanilla. Pour into hot jars, leaving 1/4 inch space at the
top. Secure lids; process in a boiling water bath for 10 minutes. Makes
4 pints.

Make hand-dipped waffle cones to give with
Praline Ice Cream Syrup. Just dip the top half of waffle cones
in melted chocolate chips, then roll them in chopped peanuts
or colorful sprinkles.

cakes, pies & more!

Hot Fudge Sauce

Serve warm over icy bowls of vanilla ice cream, slices of cheesecake or chunks of fresh fruit.

3/4 c. semi-sweet chocolate
   chips
1/4 c. butter

2/3 c. sugar
2/3 c. evaporated milk

Melt chocolate chips and butter in a heavy saucepan over low heat, stirring constantly; mix in sugar and milk. Bring mixture to a boil; reduce heat and boil over low heat for 8 minutes, stirring frequently. Remove from heat; cool slightly. Store in an airtight container in the refrigerator for up to 5 days. Makes about 1-1/2 cups.

Celebrate Summer! Surprise friends with their very own ice cream kit. Include jars of Hot Fudge Sauce and Praline Ice Cream Syrup, an ice cream scoop, sugar cones and lots of sprinkles. Don't forget a jar of cherries!

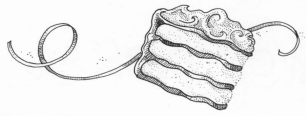

Strawberry Pie

Arrange sliced strawberries on top in a star shape...line blueberries around the edges for a perfect patriotic dessert.

4 c. strawberries, hulled and
    sliced
9-inch pie crust, baked
1-1/2 c. water
3/4 c. sugar

2 T. cornstarch
3-oz. box strawberry gelatin mix
Optional: frozen whipped
    topping, thawed

Spread strawberries in pie crust; set aside. Whisk water, sugar and cornstarch together in a small saucepan; bring to a boil over medium heat. Boil until clear and thick, about 2 minutes. Remove from heat; stir in gelatin until dissolved. Pour over berries in pie crust; refrigerate until firm. Spread with whipped topping before serving, if desired. Serves 8.

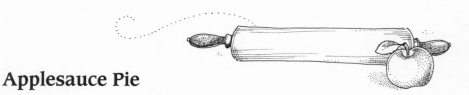

Applesauce Pie

An Amish recipe bursting with flavor.

1 c. sugar
2 T. all-purpose flour
1 t. nutmeg
1/2 t. cinnamon
2 eggs, slightly beaten
1/2 c. butter, melted

1 c. chunky unsweetened
    applesauce
1 t. vanilla extract
2 T. lemon juice
9-inch pie crust

Combine first 4 ingredients in a mixing bowl; blend in eggs. Add the next 4 ingredients; mix gently and set aside. Arrange pie crust in an ungreased 9" pie pan; pour in applesauce mixture. Bake at 350 degrees for 45 minutes; let cool to room temperature. Makes 8 servings.

cakes, pies & more!

Chocolate-Raspberry Cream Pie

The classic combination of chocolate and raspberry is a taste that everyone loves.

1-1/2 c. chocolate wafers,
   crushed
3 T. butter, melted
2 c. whipping cream
1/2 c. sugar

1 t. vanilla extract
1/2 c. raspberry syrup
9-oz. pkg. chocolate wafers
1/4 c. mini chocolate chips

Combine crushed cookies and butter; press into an ungreased 9" pie pan. Refrigerate until firm. Blend whipping cream until soft peaks form; gradually add sugar and vanilla, blending constantly. Stir in raspberry syrup; spread 1/2-inch thick layer in bottom of pie crust. Layer with wafers; repeat layers twice and finish with a layer of whipped topping. Cover carefully; refrigerate at least 12 hours. Sprinkle with chocolate chips before serving. Makes 8 servings.

Freeze to please! Make treats ahead of time and keep them frozen for last-minute gifts. Freeze pies up to 4 months, breads up to 3 months, cheesecakes up to 30 days and baked, unfrosted cookies up to 6 months. Be sure they are airtight, labeled and dated.

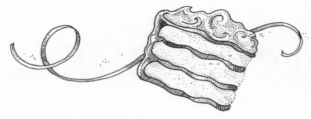

Peanut Butter Tarts

Bite-size goodies just right for snacking.

18-oz. tube refrigerated peanut butter cookie dough
1 c. semi-sweet chocolate chips

1/2 c. sweetened condensed milk
1/4 c. peanuts, finely chopped

Separate dough into 12 equal pieces; cut each into 4 equal slices and roll slices into balls. Place balls in lightly greased mini muffin cups; bake at 350 degrees for 9 minutes. Remove from oven; indent each ball using the back of a rounded 1/2 teaspoon measuring spoon. Bake 2 additional minutes; cool 15 minutes. Remove tarts from muffin cups; cool completely on wire racks. Heat chocolate chips and milk in a heavy saucepan until melted and smooth; stir often. Spoon into tarts; sprinkle with peanuts. Cool. Makes 4 dozen.

Can't be with a loved one on their birthday? You can still celebrate by sending a fun-filled birthday box. Fill a box with homemade cupcakes or a jar mix, candles and birthday cards signed by the whole gang...tuck filled balloons inside the box to hold everything in place!

cakes, pies & more!

Black-Bottom Cupcakes

A moist chocolate cupcake with a creamy vanilla center.

1-1/2 c. all-purpose flour
1 c. sugar
1/4 c. baking cocoa
1 t. baking soda
1/2 t. salt

1 c. water
1/3 c. oil
1 T. white vinegar
1 T. vanilla extract

Sift together first 5 ingredients in a mixing bowl. Combine remaining ingredients in a separate bowl; pour into the dry ingredients. Stir batter until well blended. Fill paper-lined muffin cups 1/2 full with batter. Drop one tablespoonful filling into each cup. Use a spoon to lightly cover the filling with the remaining cupcake batter. Bake at 350 degrees for 30 to 35 minutes. Makes 1-1/2 dozen.

Filling:

8-oz. pkg. cream cheese,
    softened
1 egg
1/3 c. sugar

1/4 t. salt
1/2 t. vanilla extract
1 c. mini chocolate chips

Blend together first 5 ingredients until smooth. Stir in chocolate chips.

Give a batch of Black-Bottom Cupcakes with a can of cherry pie filling...tie on some new measuring spoons so friends can top off cupcakes with a teaspoon of cherries!

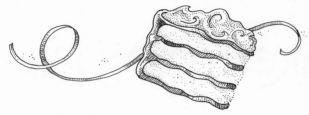

All-Star Apple Pie in a Jar

A handy pie filling to have on hand any time of year.

4-1/2 c. sugar
1 c. cornstarch
2-1/2 t. cinnamon
1/4 t. nutmeg
1/8 t. ground cloves
1 t. salt

10 c. water
3 T. lemon juice
8 to 10 lbs. apples, cored, peeled
   and sliced
7 1-quart, wide-mouth canning
   jars and lids, sterilized

Combine first 7 ingredients in a large saucepan; heat over high heat until thick and bubbly, stirring often. Remove from heat; stir in lemon juice and set aside. Pack apple slices into prepared jars; slowly pour syrup mixture over apples, covering them completely. Gently tap jars to release air bubbles; wipe rims. Secure with sterilized lids and rings; process jars in a boiling water bath for 30 minutes, completely submerging jars in boiling water. Set jars aside to cool; once cool, press top of each lid, ensuring the seal is tight and the lid does not move up or down. Makes 7 jars.

Top of the class! Paint the top of the lid for All-Star Apple Pie in a Jar with 2 coats of chalkboard paint, allowing to dry in between. Then just use chalk to write a message or draw designs on top...A+!

cakes, pies & more!

Mug-nificent Chocolate-Cherry Cake Mixes

The ideal mix to surprise college students away from home.

18-1/2 oz. pkg. chocolate cake
   mix
3.4-oz. pkg. instant chocolate
   pudding mix
16 plastic zipping bags

2-2/3 c. powdered sugar, divided
12 t. cherry drink mix, divided
8 12-oz. microwave-safe
   coffee mugs

Place cake mix and pudding mix in a large bowl, blend well with a wire whisk. Place 1/2 cup dry mix into 8 plastic zipping bags; smooth each bag to remove as much air as possible before sealing. Label each bag "Cake Mix." Place 1/3 cup powdered sugar and 1-1/2 teaspoons drink mix in each remaining bag; label these bags "Glaze Mix." Place one of each mix into each mug. Attach a gift tag with instructions to cups. Makes 8.

Instructions:

Generously coat inside of mug with non-stick vegetable spray. Empty Cake Mix into mug. Add one egg white, one tablespoon oil and one tablespoon water; stir well until combined. Microwave on high for 2 minutes. While cake is cooking, place Glaze Mix into a small bowl; add 1-1/2 teaspoons water and mix well. Pour glaze over warm cake.

Tea-rific! Place Mug-nificent Chocolate-Cherry Cake Mixes inside teacups instead of mugs...fun to give away at showers and tea parties.

Refreshing Pear Cake

Your kitchen will smell wonderful while this moist cake is baking!

4 c. pears, cored, peeled and
  chopped
2 c. sugar
3 c. all-purpose flour
1 t. salt
1-1/2 t. baking soda

1 t. nutmeg
1 t. cinnamon
1/2 t. ground cloves
4 egg whites, slightly beaten
2/3 c. oil

Combine pears and sugar in a large mixing bowl; set aside for one hour. Mix flour, salt, baking soda and spices together; set aside. Blend egg whites and oil into pear mixture; gradually mix in flour mixture. Pour batter into a lightly greased 10" Bundt® pan; bake at 325 degrees for 60 to 70 minutes. Cool in pan for 10 minutes; loosen sides and remove from pan to cool completely. Makes 10 to 12 servings.

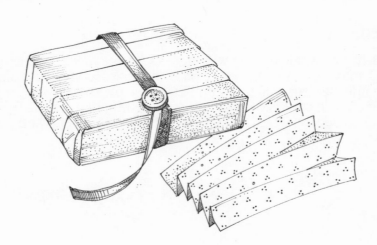

So pretty! When wrapping a boxed cake, start by covering it
in plain wrapping or tissue paper. Then fold a strip of
coordinating tissue paper into several pleats and wrap it
around the middle, taping in back.

cakes, pies & more!

Jammin' Blackberry Cake

An old-fashioned mile-high cake friends & family are sure to enjoy.

3/4 c. butter, softened
1 c. sugar
6 eggs
3 c. all-purpose flour
1 t. baking soda
1 T. cinnamon

1 T. allspice
1 t. ground cloves
1 c. buttermilk
1-1/4 c. seedless blackberry jam
2 16-oz. containers cream
   cheese frosting

Cream butter and sugar in a large mixing bowl; blend in eggs, one at a time. Set aside. Combine flour, baking soda and spices together; mix into sugar mixture alternately with buttermilk. Stir in blackberry jam; pour into 3 greased and floured 9" round baking pans. Bake at 325 degrees for 25 to 30 minutes or until a toothpick inserted into the centers removes clean; cool in pans for 10 minutes. Remove from pans; cool completely. Arrange one layer on a serving plate; frost sides and top. Layer with second cake; frost sides and top. Repeat with remaining cake. Makes 16 servings.

Top Jammin' Blackberry Cake with edible spring flowers, non-pareils, a cinnamon-sugar stencil or a border of fresh blackberries...a delightful Mothers' Day surprise.

Caramelized Apple Tart Triangles

Simply the best when topped with a scoop of vanilla ice cream.

1 T. butter
3 c. apples, cored, peeled and
    thinly sliced
3/4 c. sugar, divided
2 eggs
2 T. all-purpose flour

2 T. lemon juice
1 T. water
1/4 t. baking powder
1/2 t. cinnamon
1/4 c. sliced almonds, toasted

Melt butter in a 12" skillet; add apple slices and 1/4 cup sugar. Sauté until apples are golden; remove from heat and set aside. Combine eggs, remaining sugar, flour, lemon juice, water, baking powder and cinnamon; blend well. Arrange apple slices in a buttered 9" pie pan; sprinkle with almonds. Pour batter over the top; spread evenly. Bake at 350 degrees until golden, about 20 minutes; set aside for at least 15 minutes. Slice into wedges; serve warm or cold. Makes 8 servings.

Wrapping paper designed by children sends extra love with gifts from the kitchen to grandparents, aunts and uncles. Use recent drawings as the wrapping or photocopy them onto colored paper and tie on a rick-rack bow.

cakes, pies & more!

Bite-Size Cheesecake Treats

Blueberry or raspberry pie filling make tasty mini cheesecakes too!

12-oz. pkg. vanilla wafers,
    crushed
2 8-oz. pkgs. cream cheese,
    softened

3/4 c. sugar
2 eggs
1 t. vanilla extract
21-oz. can cherry pie filling

Place 1/2 teaspoon crushed vanilla wafers into 48 paper-lined mini muffin cups; set aside. With an electric mixer, blend together cream cheese, sugar, eggs and vanilla. Pour mixture evenly into muffin cups, filling almost to the top. Bake at 350 degrees for 15 minutes. Cool completely. Top each with a teaspoonful of pie filling. Makes 4 dozen.

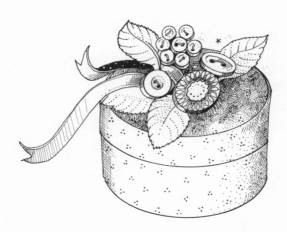

Dress up a package of Bite-Size Cheesecake Treats with a
dainty button bouquet. Gather a few unique buttons
and thread each with green floral wire for a "stem."
Add a few small silk leaves, and tie it all together
with a tiny green ribbon.

Perfect Pecan Pie

So easy to prepare...it's not just for Thanksgiving anymore!

3 eggs
3/4 c. sugar
1 c. corn syrup
3 T. butter, melted

1/4 t. salt
1 t. vanilla extract
1-1/2 c. chopped pecans
9-inch pie crust

Blend eggs and sugar together; add next 4 ingredients. Mix well; fold in pecans. Set pie crust into an ungreased 9" pie pan; spread pecan mixture into crust. Place on a rimmed baking sheet; bake at 400 degrees on the lower rack of the oven for 15 minutes. Reduce heat to 325 degrees; continue baking for 40 to 45 minutes, shielding crust with aluminum foil. Cool on a wire rack. Makes 8 servings.

No-Fail Peanut Butter Pie

For the kid in everyone...spread a thin layer of grape jelly on the pie crust before filling for a peanut butter & jelly delight.

5-oz. pkg. instant vanilla
    pudding mix
2 c. milk
1/2 c. whipping cream, whipped
1-1/3 c. creamy peanut butter

9-inch pie crust, baked
8-oz. container frozen whipped
    topping, thawed
Garnish: chocolate syrup and
    chopped peanuts

Whisk pudding mix and milk together until smooth and creamy; add whipped cream and peanut butter. Whisk until completely blended; pour into pie crust. Spread with whipped topping; place in freezer for one hour. Cover and refrigerate for 2 hours. Drizzle with chocolate syrup and sprinkle with chopped peanuts before serving. Serves 8.

cakes, pies & more!

Have-On-Hand Pie Crust Mix

*Use 2-1/2 cups mix and 5 to 7 tablespoons cold water
for a 2-crust pie or 1-1/2 cups mix and 2 to 3 tablespoons
cold water for a one-crust pie.*

12 c. all-purpose flour   5 c. shortening
2-1/2 T. salt

Sift flour and salt together twice; gradually cut in shortening with a
pastry cutter until coarse crumbs form. Store in an airtight container in
a cool place for up to 6 weeks. Attach instructions before giving.
Makes about 16 single pie crusts.

Instructions:

Stir water into pie crust mix until pastry holds together; roll out on a
lightly floured surface into a circle large enough to fit the pie plate.
Prick the bottom and sides of a one-crust pie before baking; vent the
top crust of a 2-crust pie before baking. For recipes using a pre-baked
crust, bake at 400 degrees until golden, about 10 minutes.

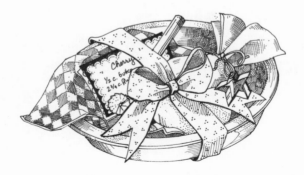

A pie baking gift set! Nestle a pastry cutter, a package of
Have-On-Hand Pie Crust Mix and a mini cookie cutter
(for top crust designs) inside a new pie plate. Give with a
rolling pin and your favorite pie recipes.

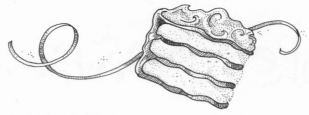

Coconut Snack Cake

Wrap individual squares in wax paper...just right for bake sales.

2 c. all-purpose flour
1 t. baking soda
2 t. cinnamon, divided
1/2 t. salt
2/3 c. shortening
1 c. brown sugar, packed
2 eggs

1 t. vanilla extract
1 c. buttermilk
1 c. flaked coconut
1 c. sugar
1/2 t. nutmeg
1/4 c. light cream

Sift together flour, baking soda, one teaspoon cinnamon and salt; set aside. Cream shortening and brown sugar until light and fluffy. Blend in eggs, one at a time, blending well after each addition; mix in vanilla. Add dry ingredients alternately with buttermilk. Spread batter into a greased 13"x9" baking pan. Combine remaining ingredients; sprinkle over batter. Bake at 350 degrees for 35 minutes or until center tests done. Cool on wire rack. Makes 12 to 15 servings.

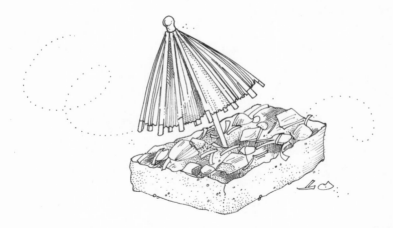

Too cute! Top squares of Coconut Snack Cake with dried pineapple bits and mini paper umbrellas...give to friends headed off to the beach or take to the next summertime picnic.

cakes, pies & more!

Fudge Brownie Pie

Use melted white chocolate chips to pipe on designs or sprinkle marshmallows on top right after baking.

23-oz. pkg. brownie mix
1/2 c. water
1 egg

2/3 c. chopped walnuts
9-inch pie crust

Combine brownie mix, water and egg; beat until smooth. Fold in nuts. Pour mixture into pie crust. Bake at 350 degrees for 35 to 40 minutes or until center tests done. Cool on a wire rack. Serves 6 to 8.

Chocolatey Chip Pie

For extra chocolate, stir in 1/2 cup candy-coated chocolates along with the chocolate chips.

1/2 c. all-purpose flour
1/2 c. sugar
1/2 c. brown sugar, packed
2 eggs, beaten

1 c. butter, melted
6-oz. pkg. chocolate chips
9-inch pie crust

Mix together flour and sugars; blend in eggs. Mix in cooled butter; stir in chocolate chips. Pour mixture into pie crust; bake at 325 for one hour. Cool on a wire rack. Serves 6 to 8.

Fudge Brownie Pie and Chocolatey Chip Pie are fun alternatives to birthday cake...and they both go great with ice cream!

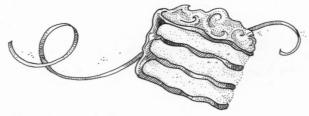

Ambrosia Cream Pie

Just like the salad Grandma always makes.

11-oz. can mandarin oranges,
   drained and chopped
8-oz. can crushed pineapple,
   drained
1 c. milk
3.4-oz. pkg. instant vanilla
   pudding mix

1 c. frozen whipped topping,
   thawed
1 c. flaked coconut
9-inch graham cracker pie crust
Garnish: whipped topping and
   toasted flaked coconut

Lightly press chopped mandarin oranges and pineapple between
several layers of paper towels to remove excess juice; set aside.
Combine milk and vanilla pudding mix; add whipped topping, mixing
well. Stir in coconut, oranges and pineapple; spread into pie crust.
Cover and refrigerate until firm, about 6 hours or overnight. Garnish
with additional whipped topping and toasted coconut before serving.
Makes 8 servings.

Ambrosia Cream Pie looks so pretty presented in a nostalgic
milk glass pie plate. Wrap it up in clear cellophane and use a
favorite black & white photo for a gift tag...attach it with a
satin ribbon and a vintage dress buckle.

A Gift from Me!

HoMeMade GooDies from:

Make a copy of these little tags & tie them on for extra special gifts.

The good things in Life are not to be had singly; but come to us in a mixture.

~anonymous

So WHAT'S FOR DESSert!

homemade by:

MMMMM GOOD
IF · I · DO · SAY · SO · MYSELF!

Place a mix inside a recipe box... 2 gifts for the kitchen!

Deliver slices of fruity breads in berry baskets.

Breads & Spreads

Stack mini jars of several spreads & give with a loaf of homemade bread.

Fill a rustic basket with muffins & deliver with an assortment of flavored butters.

Line a vintage pail with a kitchen towel & tuck freshly baked breadsticks inside.

Pumpkin Bread in a Jar

*No jars on hand? Pour the batter into a well-greased 9"x5" loaf pan
and bake at 350 degrees for 50 to 55 minutes.*

2 c. all-purpose flour
2 t. baking powder
1/2 t. baking soda
1 t. cinnamon
1/2 t. nutmeg
1/2 t. allspice
1 t. salt
1 c. canned pumpkin

1 c. sugar
1/2 c. milk
2 eggs
1/4 c. butter, softened
1/2 c. chopped pecans
5 1-quart, wide-mouth canning
  jars and lids, sterilized

Combine first 7 ingredients together; set aside. Blend pumpkin, sugar,
milk and eggs together in a large mixing bowl; add dry ingredients and
butter, mixing well. Fold in pecans. Pour equally into greased jars,
filling halfway with batter. Wipe jar rims; bake at 325 degrees for
45 minutes or until a toothpick inserted in the center removes clean.
Remove jars from oven; wipe rims clean. Secure sterilized lids with
rings; set aside to cool. Check for seals; store sealed jars in the
refrigerator for up to 6 weeks. Makes 4 to 5 jars.

Trick-or-treat! Use yellow construction paper to cut out
Jack-'O-Lantern eyes, a nose and a mouth and glue them to
the front of Pumpkin Bread in a Jar.

breads & spreads

Celebration Cherry Bread Mix

Turn this mix into a hearty raisin bread...simply substitute raisins for dried cherries and cranberries and add another 1/2 teaspoon of cinnamon.

2-1/2 c. all-purpose flour
1 t. baking powder
1 t. baking soda
1 t. cinnamon
1/4 t. nutmeg
1/2 t. salt

1 c. quick-cooking oats, uncooked
3/4 c. dried cherries
3/4 c. sweetened, dried cranberries

Combine flour, baking powder, baking soda, cinnamon, nutmeg and salt together in a large mixing bowl; mix well. Add remaining ingredients; toss until blended. Place mixture in a plastic zipping bag or other airtight container; attach instructions. Store in a cool, dry place.

Instructions:

Whisk 3/4 cup honey, 3/4 cup milk, 3/4 cup melted butter and 2 beaten eggs together; set aside. Place mix in a large mixing bowl; add honey mixture, stirring until just moistened. Pour batter equally into 2 greased 8"x4" loaf pans; bake at 350 degrees for 35 to 40 minutes or until a toothpick inserted in the center removes clean. Cool on wire rack. Serves 16.

Bring a special gift to the next big celebration. Purchase a blank journal and fill in pages with a fun theme like, "50 Fun Memories" for a 50th anniversary party or "40 Reasons You're the Best" for a 40th birthday. Add stickers, drawings and photos...they'll treasure it forever!

Honey-Spice Spread

A tasty muffin spread...attach a honey server with a big homespun bow tied around the lid.

12-oz. jar honey   2 whole cloves
3-inch cinnamon stick   2 whole allspice

Pour honey into a slightly larger jar; add remaining ingredients. Set in a bowl of very hot water that covers at least 3/4 of the jar for 20 minutes; remove from bowl. Secure lid. Makes 1-1/2 cups.

Blueberry-Honey Spread

Delicious on English muffins and bagels.

1/2 c. frozen blueberries, thawed   1/4 c. honey, divided
1/2 c. butter, softened   1 t. cinnamon

Combine blueberries, butter and 2 tablespoons honey in a small saucepan; bring to a boil over medium heat, stirring constantly. Reduce heat; simmer until thickened and reduced by about half. Cool. Blend in cinnamon and remaining honey; serve warm. Store in an airtight container in the refrigerator. Makes about one cup.

Wrap a doily around a loaf of bread, tie with a fluffy sheer bow and deliver with a crock of homemade spread to the tea party hostess.

breads & spreads

On-the-Go Muffin Mix

Even the busiest families can enjoy these homebaked goodies.

2 c. all-purpose flour
1-1/2 t. baking powder
1/2 t. baking soda
1 t. cinnamon

1/2 t. nutmeg
1/2 t. vanilla powder
1/8 t. salt
2/3 c. brown sugar, packed

Combine the first 7 ingredients; spoon into an airtight container. Place brown sugar in a plastic zipping bag; place on top of flour mixture. Secure lid; attach instructions.

Instructions:

Place mix in a medium mixing bowl, laying plastic bag to the side; set bowl aside. Blend 3/4 cup buttermilk, 3/4 cup applesauce, brown sugar, one egg and 1-1/2 tablespoons oil together until frothy, about 2 minutes. Form a well in the center of the dry ingredients; pour in buttermilk mixture, stirring until just moistened. Spoon batter into greased or paper-lined muffin cups filling 2/3 full; bake at 350 degrees for 20 minutes. Cool in pan on a wire rack for 12 minutes before removing from muffin cups. Makes 12.

cranberries   white chocolate   chunks   walnuts   raisins

Make On-the-Go Muffin Mix everyone's favorite by adding 1/2 cup dried cranberries, white chocolate chips, chocolate chunks, walnuts or raisins...place them in a plastic bag and tie onto the jar to stir in before baking.

Sweet & Spicy Pear Spread

Use as a spread for muffins and breads or pour over softened cream cheese and serve with crackers as an appetizer.

2 c. dried pear halves, chopped
1 c. sweet onion, minced
2-1/2 c. pear nectar
2 c. raisins
3/4 c. cider vinegar
1/2 c. dried tart cherries
1/3 c. sugar
1 T. mustard seed

1 T. fresh ginger, peeled and
grated
1/4 t. salt
1/8 t. nutmeg
4-inch cinnamon stick
1 c. water
6 1/2-pint jars and lids

Combine ingredients in a 4-quart saucepan; heat to boiling over high heat, stirring occasionally; reduce heat to low and simmer until pears are soft, about 15 minutes. Discard cinnamon stick; spoon into jars for gift giving. Refrigerate for up to one month. Makes 6 cups.

Bring a gift for the brunch host.
Pour Sweet & Spicy Pear Spread inside a
simple lidded glass bowl...tie on an oversized ribbon to keep
the lid secure and tuck a serving spoon into the knot.

breads & spreads

Almond-Pear Muffins

Pastry-like muffins with a honey-cream spread.

1-1/4 c. all-purpose flour
3/4 c. brown sugar, packed
1 T. baking powder
1 t. ground ginger, divided
1/2 t. salt
1 c. pears, chopped
1 c. whole-bran cereal

1 c. milk
1 egg
1/4 c. oil
2 T. chopped almonds
8-oz. pkg. cream cheese,
 softened
1 T. honey

Combine flour, brown sugar, baking powder, 1/2 teaspoon ginger and salt in a large mixing bowl; stir in pears and set aside. Mix cereal and milk together; set aside for 5 minutes. Add egg and oil to cereal mixture; mix into pear mixture until just moistened. Fill greased or paper-lined muffin cups 3/4 full with batter; sprinkle tops with almonds. Bake at 400 degrees for 18 to 20 minutes; cool. Blend cream cheese, honey and remaining ginger together; serve with muffins as a spread. Makes 12 to 16 servings.

Make a sweet toast to
family & friends at the next
breakfast or brunch gathering.
Just bake Almond-Pear Muffins in
paper-lined mini muffin cups...stack
3 to 4 in a clear fluted glass and set
at each place setting. Charming!

Whole-Wheat Baking Mix

*Easy to use within a month with so many tasty
recipes right at your fingertips.*

4 c. all-purpose flour
4 c. whole-wheat flour
1/4 c. baking powder

2-1/2 t. salt
1-2/3 c. powdered milk
1-3/4 c. shortening

Combine first 5 ingredients in a large mixing bowl; cut in shortening with a pastry blender until coarse crumbs form. Place in a glass airtight container; store in a cool place. Use within one month. Attach instructions. Makes about 10 cups.

Whole-Wheat Pancakes

Whisk one egg and one cup water together in a mixing bowl; stir in 2-1/4 cups Whole-Wheat Baking Mix until just moistened. Drop by heaping tablespoonfuls onto a greased hot griddle; flip when bubbles form along the edge until both sides are golden. Makes about one dozen.

Fill a new glass canister with Whole-Wheat Baking Mix
and tuck an old-fashioned measuring scoop inside.
Be sure to tie on all the breakfast recipes that use the mix.

breads & spreads

Whole-Wheat Coffee Cake

Blend one egg with 1/2 cup water; stir in 2-1/4 cups Whole-Wheat Baking Mix. Fold in 1/2 cup raisins; spread batter in a greased 13"x9" baking pan. Set aside. Combine 1/4 cup packed brown sugar and 1/2 cup all-purpose flour; cut in 1/2 cup butter with a pastry blender until coarse crumbs form. Sprinkle on top of batter; bake at 400 degrees for 25 minutes. Cut into squares; serve warm. Makes 12 to 15 servings.

Whole-Wheat Muffins

Whisk one egg and 1-1/4 cups water together in a large mixing bowl; Stir in 4-1/2 cups Whole-Wheat Baking Mix until just moistened. Fill greased muffin cups 2/3 full with batter; bake at 400 degrees for 15 to 20 minutes. Makes about 1-1/2 dozen.

Special Delivery! Copy vintage postcards and old letters onto plain paper for easy personalized wrapping. Use a twisted cord or jute as ribbon and tie on a shipping label for the gift tag.

Maple Syrup

Use dark corn syrup for the best color and flavor...wonderful over warm pancakes or waffles.

2 c. water
1 c. sugar
2 c. corn syrup

1/4 t. salt
1-1/2 t. maple flavoring

Combine the first 4 ingredients in a saucepan; heat over medium heat until mixture reaches a rolling boil, stirring occasionally. Boil for 7 minutes; remove from heat and set aside for 15 minutes. Stir in maple flavoring; set aside to cool to room temperature. Store in an airtight container in the refrigerator. Makes about 4 cups.

Doughnut Muffins

Puts the "good" in good morning!

1/3 c. shortening
1/2 c. sugar
1 egg
1/2 t. vanilla extract
1-1/2 c. all-purpose flour

1-1/2 t. baking powder
1/2 t. salt
1/2 c. milk
Garnish: powdered sugar

Cream shortening and sugar; add egg and vanilla extract, blending well. Set aside. Combine flour, baking powder and salt; add to egg mixture alternately with milk, blending after each addition. Fill greased muffin cups 2/3 full with batter; bake at 350 degrees for 20 minutes or until a toothpick inserted in the center removes clean. Cool to warm. Place powdered sugar in a paper bag; add muffins and shake to coat. Makes 12.

breads & spreads

Cinnamon Pancake Mix to Flip Over

Pancakes for breakfast, lunch or dinner are oh-so easy when this mix is ready and waiting in the fridge.

4 c. quick-cooking oats, uncooked
2 c. all-purpose flour
2 c. whole-wheat flour
1 c. powdered milk

2 to 3 T. cinnamon
1-1/2 T. salt
3 T. baking powder
1/2 t. cream of tartar

Combine ingredients; place in an airtight container. Attach instructions; store in the refrigerator. Makes about 8 cups.

Instructions:

Blend 2 eggs in a large mixing bowl until frothy; gradually mix in 1/3 cup oil. Add 2 cups pancake mix alternately with one cup water; mix well. Heat batter by 1/4 cupfuls on a lightly greased, hot griddle until both sides are golden, flipping once when bubbles form along the edge. Makes 12 servings.

Create a clever package for Cinnamon Pancake Mix to Flip Over. Fold a bright kitchen towel in half and sew 2 sides closed to form a bag...slip the mix inside and tie closed with jute. Don't forget to give with a big spatula for flipping!

Tutti Fruity Syrup

Smilin' strawberry or lip smackin' lemon syrup...let your children decide the flavor of the day!

3-oz. box strawberry gelatin mix   2 c. corn syrup
1/2 c. boiling water

Dissolve half the gelatin in boiling water, reserving remaining half for use in another recipe; stir in corn syrup. Serve warm or cold; store refrigerated in an airtight container. Makes 2-1/2 cups.

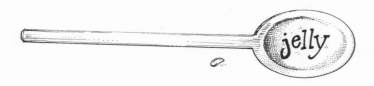

Easiest Raspberry Jelly

Spread over pancakes, waffles or even pound cake...stir a spoonful into a warm mug of coffee for a tasty treat.

.22-oz. pkg. unsweetened   1.75-oz. box light fruit
  raspberry drink mix   powdered pectin
3 c. water   3 c. sugar

Stir drink mix into water until dissolved; set aside. Combine powdered pectin with 1/2 cup raspberry mixture; gradually stir in sugar and remaining raspberry mix. Pour into airtight containers; let stand at room temperature overnight. Store in the refrigerator. Makes 4 cups.

Use different drink mixes to vary flavors of
Easiest Raspberry Jelly...try making strawberry and
orange and layer them into old-fashioned jelly jars.

breads & spreads

Strawberry-Banana Bread

Just right for breakfast...or a tasty midnight snack.

2 c. strawberries, hulled, sliced
   and divided
1 c. all-purpose flour
3/4 c. whole-wheat pastry flour
1 t. baking soda
1 t. salt

1/4 t. baking powder
1/2 c. sugar
1/4 t. nutmeg
2/3 c. bananas, mashed
2 egg whites, beaten
1/3 c. water

Place half the strawberries in a saucepan and crush with a fork; simmer over medium heat for 2 minutes, stirring constantly. Remove from heat; stir in remaining sliced strawberries. Refrigerate. Combine flours, baking soda, salt and baking powder; set aside. Place sugar and nutmeg in a large mixing bowl; mix in bananas. Add egg whites and water; mix well. Blend in flour mixture; fold in strawberries. Spread in a greased 9"x5" loaf pan; bake at 350 degrees for 40 to 60 minutes or until a toothpick inserted in the center removes clean. Cool in pan for 10 minutes; remove loaf from pan to cool completely on a wire rack. Makes 8 servings.

Try baking Strawberry-Banana Bread in 3-inch terra cotta pots for individual gifts. To prepare pots, coat insides with oil and bake at 350 degrees for 30 minutes; cool completely then repeat process again. Pour bread batter into foil-lined pots and bake as directed, reducing time by 10 to 15 minutes.

Simply Bread

Not sure what's better, the aroma of bread baking or the first warm bite…if jam is involved, it's no contest!

2 c. all-purpose flour
3 c. whole-wheat flour
1 T. sugar

1 T. plus 1/2 t. active dry yeast
2-1/2 c. warm water

Combine first 3 ingredients together; set aside. Sprinkle yeast over warm water; set aside until bubbly. Pour into a large mixing bowl; gradually mix in 4 cups flour mixture. Knead dough while adding the remaining flour until dough is smooth and elastic, about 5 to 8 minutes. Place in a greased bowl; turning once to coat both sides. Cover; let rise until double in bulk. Punch dough down; shape into a loaf and place in a 9"x5" loaf pan. Cover and let rise until double in bulk; bake at 375 degrees until golden, about 45 minutes. Makes 8 servings.

Use monogrammed linen napkins to wrap up several different loaves of bread…place the loaf in the middle, bring the corners up and tie with a bow, being sure the monogram can be seen. Place the wrapped loaves in a cheerful bread basket and deliver to newlyweds in their new home.

breads & spreads

Better-Than-Ever Bread Bowls

Fill the bread bowls with muffins to give away and save the removed bread for yourself...it's wonderful with cheese or dill dip!

2 pkgs. active dry yeast
1 T. sugar
1-3/4 c. plus 2 T. warm water, divided
2 c. whole-wheat flour

2 c. bread flour, divided
2 t. salt
1 egg white
2 T. water
1 T. coarse salt

Stir yeast and sugar into 1-3/4 cup warm water; let stand until creamy, about 10 minutes. Pour into a large mixing bowl; add wheat flour, one cup bread flour and salt, mixing well. Knead in remaining flour until dough is smooth and elastic, about 8 minutes; place in a greased bowl, turning once to coat all sides. Cover and let rise until double in bulk; punch dough down and set aside for 10 minutes. Divide into 4 portions; place on ungreased baking sheets. Flatten slightly; cover and let rise until double in bulk. Whisk egg white and remaining water together in a small bowl; brush over loaves. Sprinkle with coarse salt; bake at 375 degrees for 40 to 50 minutes or until golden. Remove and let cool; hollow out loaves leaving a one-inch shell to form bowls. Makes 4.

Fill Better-Than-Ever Bread Bowls with chili seasoning, cornbread muffins, plastic spoons and a few bandannas for napkins. The chili can be served right in the bread bowl!

Easy Cheesy Spread

Delicious with crackers or a loaf of crusty bread.

16-oz. pkg. pasteurized
    processed cheese spread
3-oz. can evaporated milk
1 T. vinegar

1/2 t. garlic salt
1/2 t. dry mustard
3 1/2-pint canning jars and lids,
    sterilized

Melt cheese spread with milk in a double boiler; stir until smooth and creamy. Remove from heat; stir in remaining ingredients. Fill jars 3/4 full; secure lids. Place in a boiling water bath for 10 minutes; set aside to cool. Check lids for seals. Makes 3 jars.

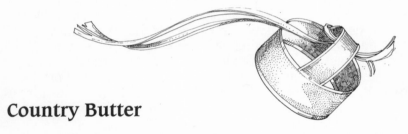

Country Butter

Guests have a sweet tooth? Stir in a teaspoon of cinnamon or apple pie spice.

2 c. butter, softened
1 c. buttermilk

3/4 c. oil
1/4 t. salt

Blend ingredients until creamy in a food processor; place in an airtight container. Refrigerate until chilled; cover and store in the refrigerator. Makes about 3 cups.

Tie a vintage-style biscuit cutter on a container of
Country Butter...an old-fashioned surprise sure to
bring smiles.

breads & spreads

Presto-Pesto Spread

Mix up a day or 2 ahead of time and refrigerate to allow flavors to blend. Let sit at room temperature for about 30 minutes before serving.

8-oz. pkg. cream cheese, softened
2 t. chopped pimento

7-oz. container refrigerated pesto sauce

Cream ingredients together; spoon into an airtight container. Cover and refrigerate until serving. Store in refrigerator for up to one week. Makes 1-1/2 cups.

Turn a chip & dip bowl into a bread & spread server! Just put a container of Presto-Pesto Spread in the middle (where the dip usually goes) and surround it with toasted slices of baguette bread. Cover it all with plastic wrap and take it along to your next neighborhood gathering.

Golden Hushpuppy Mix

Most people think hushpuppies are hard to make, but with this easy mix, these tasty tidbits can be enjoyed in 3 easy steps.

1-1/2 c. cornmeal
3/4 c. all-purpose flour
3 T. dried, minced onion
1 t. baking powder

1-1/2 t. sugar
1 t. salt
1/2 t. baking soda
1/2 t. cayenne pepper

Combine ingredients; mix well. Place in a plastic zipping bag. Attach instructions.

Instructions:

Combine mix with 1-1/2 cups buttermilk and one beaten egg in a medium mixing bowl; stir until well blended. Drop by tablespoonfuls into a deep skillet filled with 1-1/2 inch depth of 350 degree oil; heat until golden. Drain on paper towels; serve warm. Makes 4 servings.

Great for Fathers' Day! Tuck Golden Hushpuppy Mix
and some fish-shaped cheese crackers inside a
new tackle box...give it to your favorite fisherman
to enjoy with his next catch.

breads & spreads

Gotta-Have-It Cornbread Mix

Divide this mix into 8 equal batches to share with several friends.

6 c. all-purpose flour
6 c. cornmeal
2 c. powdered milk
1 c. sugar

1/3 c. baking powder
1 T. salt
1-1/2 c. shortening

Combine first 6 ingredients together in a large mixing bowl; cut in shortening with a pastry cutter until mixture resembles coarse crumbs. Store in an airtight container at room temperature for up to 6 weeks or freeze for up to 6 months. Attach instructions. Makes 16 cups.

Instructions:

Combine 2 cups cornbread mix with one teaspoon chili powder in a large mixing bowl; form a well in the center and set aside. Whisk one egg and 3/4 cup water together; pour into well. Mix until just combined; spread batter in a greased 8"x8" baking pan. Bake at 425 degrees for 20 to 25 minutes or until a toothpick inserted in the center removes clean. Makes 16 servings.

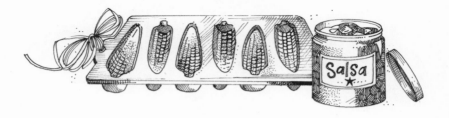

Package Gotta-Have-It Cornbread Mix with a mini cornstick pan and a jar of salsa. Add a line to instructions: "For a quick & easy appetizer, bake batter in pan, then dip tiny cornsticks into salsa." Delicious!

Berry-Delicious Country Muffin Mix

Growing a strawberry plant, blueberry or raspberry bush at home?
Give this mix with basket of fresh berries...any kind will do!

1-1/2 c. all-purpose flour
1 c. quick-cooking oats,
   uncooked

1/4 c. brown sugar, packed
1 T. baking powder
1/2 t. cinnamon

Combine the first 5 ingredients in a large mixing bowl; place in a large plastic zipping bag. Attach baking instructions.

Instructions:

Pour muffin mix in a large bowl; add one cup milk, one beaten egg and 3 tablespoons oil. Gently fold in 2-1/4 cup berries. Fill paper-lined muffin cups 2/3 full. Bake at 425 degrees until tops are golden, about 25 to 30 minutes. Makes one dozen.

Whip up some lemon butter to give with Berry-Delicious Country Muffin Mix. Just stir sugar and lemon zest into butter to taste...delightful on warm muffins.

breads & spreads

Ginger & Spice & Everything Nice Muffin Mix

A great gift for a family on the go.

1-3/4 c. all-purpose flour
2 T. sugar
1 T. baking powder
1/2 t. baking soda
1/2 t. vanilla powder

1 t. cinnamon
1/2 t. nutmeg
1/4 t. ground ginger
1/4 t. ground cloves
1/2 t. salt

Combine ingredients; place in an airtight container. Attach instructions.

Instructions:

Combine muffin mix with 1/4 cup melted butter, one egg and one cup milk; stir until just moistened. Fill greased or paper-lined muffin cups 2/3 full with batter; bake at 400 degrees for 15 minutes. Makes one dozen.

Ginger & Spice & Everything Nice MUFFIN MIX

Combine muffin mix with 1/4 cup melted butter, 1 egg and 1 cup milk; stir until just moistened. Fill greased or paper-lined muffin tins 2/3 full of batter; bake at 400° for 15 minutes. Makes 12.

Pumpkin Mini Muffin Mix

Place a couple mini muffin tins in a gift basket along with this mix...a welcome housewarming gift.

3 c. all-purpose flour
4 t. baking powder
1-1/4 t. salt
1 c. sugar

1 t. cinnamon
1 t. nutmeg
1 c. raisins
15-oz. can pumpkin

Combine all ingredients except for pumpkin in a large mixing bowl; spoon into a plastic zipping bag and seal. Place in a gift basket; add can of pumpkin. Attach instructions.

Instructions:

Pour muffin mix into a large mixing bowl; cut in 1/2 cup shortening with a pastry cutter until fine crumbs form. Add one cup pumpkin, one cup milk and 2 eggs; mix until just moistened. Fill greased or paper-lined mini muffin cups 2/3 full; bake at 400 degrees for 15 minutes. Remove to wire racks to cool. Makes about 5 dozen.

Fill a bushel basket with all the flavors of Fall...apples, squash, tiny pumpkins and gourds, a gallon of apple cider and Pumpkin Mini Muffin Mix. Tuck in a few colorful leaves before giving.

breads & spreads

Gingerbread Mix

Turn this bread into dessert...just serve with soft ice cream or whipped topping.

8 c. all-purpose flour
4 t. baking soda
2 t. baking powder
2 T. ground ginger

2 t. cinnamon
2 t. salt
1 t. nutmeg
1-1/2 c. shortening

Combine first 7 ingredients together; cut in shortening with a pastry cutter. Store mix in an airtight container in a cool place for up to 6 weeks. Attach instructions. Makes about 8 cups.

Instructions:

Place 2 cups mix in a mixing bowl; add 3/4 cup molasses, 1/3 cup buttermilk and one beaten egg. Mix well. Spread into a greased 8"x8" baking pan; bake at 375 degrees for 25 to 30 minutes. Cool and cut into squares to serve. Makes 16 servings.

Pair Gingerbread Mix with a powdered sugar duster and give with stencils to create whimsical designs on just-baked bread.

Peach Ice Cream Muffins

So many ice cream flavors...so many muffins!

1-1/2 c. self-rising flour
2 c. peach ice cream,
   softened
1 egg, beaten

2 T. oil
Garnish: jimmies and colored
   sugar

Place flour in a mixing bowl; stir in ice cream, egg and oil until just moistened. Fill greased or paper-lined muffin cups 3/4 full with batter; bake at 425 degrees for 15 to 20 minutes. Sprinkle with jimmies or colored sugar while warm. Makes one dozen.

Chocolatey Banana Muffins

Try making with chunks of chocolate bars instead of chips...bigger bites of chocolate are sure to please.

2 c. all-purpose flour
1/3 c. sugar
2 T. baking cocoa
1 T. baking powder

1 c. bananas, mashed
2/3 c. oil
1 egg, beaten
1 c. semi-sweet chocolate chips

Combine first 4 ingredients together; set aside. Blend bananas, oil and egg in a large mixing bowl; mix in flour mixture until just blended. Fold in chocolate chips; spoon batter into paper-lined muffin cups, filling 3/4 full. Bake at 425 degrees for 15 to 20 minutes; cool on wire racks. Makes one dozen.

Set a basket of muffins on a secret pal's doorstep and hang a
small daisy chain wreath from the doorknob...it's so fun
to keep them guessing!

Feel free to copy these tags and use colored pens to give them more ...ZING!

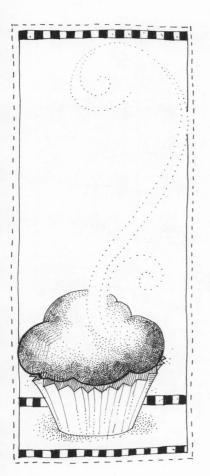

It is more blessed to give than to receive. Acts 20:35

(So NO fighting over the last muffin!)

Yummy
(IF I DO SAY SO MYSELF!)

Feel free to copy these tags on heavy paper for your gift.

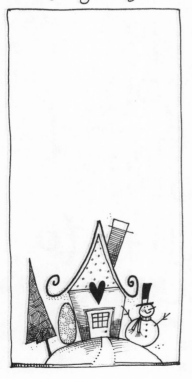

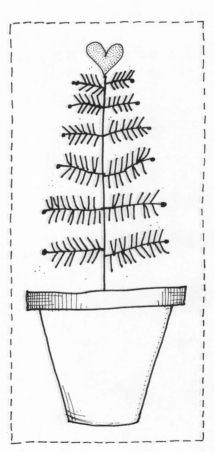

Include chips & pretzels with a dip mix.

Fill vintage shakers with seasoning blends & attach a recipe to use.

DIP DIP HOORAY!

italiana

thwestern

Sprinkle liberally on buttery popcorn, pasta, chicken or pizza.

Sauces & Seasonings

BBQ Sauce

Attach the recipe to a jar of salsa & include fresh veggies from the garden.

Salsa

Mexican Cass

Tie a pastry brush onto a jar of barbeque sauce.

Herbal DIP

Tuck an herb dip mix inside a mini watering can.

All-Season Salt Blend

Sprinkle over chicken, beef, popcorn and potato chips.

2 T. pepper
1 T. chili powder
1 T. dried parsley
1 T. garlic salt
1 T. chicken bouillon granules
1-1/2 t. onion salt

1-1/2 t. paprika
1 t. onion powder
1 t. cumin
1 t. dried marjoram
1/2 t. curry
1/3 c. salt

Combine ingredients in an airtight container; secure lid and shake to mix. Store at room temperature; use within 3 months. Makes about one cup.

Sensationally Snackable Mix

Tastes great over popcorn, mashed potatoes or warm vegetables.

3 T. butter-flavored granules
2 T. grated Parmesan cheese
1 t. dried basil

1/2 t. dried parsley
1/4 t. garlic powder
1/4 t. onion salt

Combine ingredients in an airtight container; secure lid and shake to mix. Makes about 1/3 cup.

A poppin' good time! Line a galvanized pail with paper towels, fill with popped popcorn and nestle shakers filled with All-Season Salt Blend and Sensationally Snackable Mix on top.

Sauces & Seasonings

Savory Popcorn Topper

*Keep an eye out for vintage jadite salt & pepper shakers...fill 'em
with this mix and tie a ribbon around the top with a gift tag.*

1 c. dried vegetable mix
2 t. dried oregano
2 t. dried basil
1 T. dried parsley
1 T. peppercorns

1 T. lemon zest
1 T. citric acid
1 t. garlic powder
1/4 t. celery seeds
2 dried tomatoes, thinly sliced

Combine ingredients in a food processor; blend until finely ground.
Store in an airtight container. Makes about 1/2 cup.

Tuck a shaker filled with Savory Popcorn Topper along with a
bag of microwave popcorn into an old-fashioned popcorn
container, or ask for an extra tub at the local movie theater.
Deliver with a favorite movie to a friend who may be
feeling under the weather...instant cheer!

Spaghetti Sauce Spice Blend

Add instructions to make a quick dip...just stir one cup sour cream and 1/4 cup spice blend together.

1/4 c. celery salt
1 T. dried basil
1 T. dried oregano
1 T. dried parsley

1 T. garlic powder
1 T. onion salt
1 T. sugar
1 T. pepper

Mix ingredients together; place in an airtight container. Shake before using. Attach instructions. Makes about 3/4 cup.

Instructions:

To make spaghetti sauce, whisk an 8-ounce can tomatoes with 1/4 cup spice blend in a saucepan; simmer for 30 minutes. Pour over an 8-ounce package prepared pasta. Serves 4.

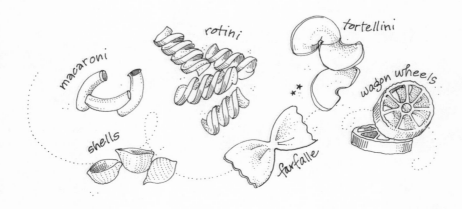

Pick your pasta! Give Spaghetti Sauce Spice Blend with a large glass jar filled with a variety of noodles...try layering macaroni, rotini, tortellini, shells and wagon wheels.

Bowl o' Bruschetta Blend

Just like the kind at the family-style Italian restaurants.

2 T. fresh basil, chopped
1/4 T. salt
1/4 c. olive oil
1/4 T. pepper

1/4 c. garlic, minced
1/3 c. sweet onion, diced
1-lb. pkg. roma tomatoes,
 chopped and seeded

Combine the ingredients in a large mixing bowl; whisk well. Pour into an airtight container and refrigerate until giving. Attach instructions. Makes 2 to 3 cups.

Instructions:

Slice one loaf round bread in half horizontally so there are 2, one-inch thick bread circles; cut each into 5 wedges. Brush with garlic-olive oil; broil until golden. Place on a serving dish; spoon bruschetta blend on top. Makes 10 servings.

Celebrate a special event Italian style! Fill a gift basket with a loaf of round bread, a bottle of garlic-olive oil and jar of Bowl o' Bruschetta Blend. Toss in a classic Italian CD to really set the mood.

pour it on!

Cranberry Salad Dressing

Add a few chopped walnuts to this salad dressing...looks great and tastes delicious!

1/2 c. cranberry juice
4 green onions, chopped
2 T. cider vinegar
2 t. Dijon mustard
1 t. maple flavoring

1/2 t. salt
1/2 t. celery seed
1/2 t. pepper
1 c. oil

Blend the first 8 ingredients together in a food processor until well mixed; slowly add oil, blending on low speed continually. Pour into an airtight container; refrigerate overnight. Shake well before serving. Makes 1-1/2 cups.

Looking for a clever way to wrap up a bottle of Cranberry Salad Dressing? Try using a document mailing tube. Simply remove the rubber ends and cut the tube to desired length. Add a whimsical design with paint pens, slip the bottle inside and replace the ends.

Sauces & Seasonings

Orchard Barbecue Sauce

Always a party pleaser...bring a jar to the next neighborhood cookout.

1 onion, minced
4 c. apple cider
1/2 c. cider vinegar
1/2 c. brown sugar, packed
1 T. mustard seed
1 t. celery salt
1/8 t. pepper

1 T. Worcestershire sauce
1 T. liquid smoke
2 12-oz. bottles chili sauce
hot pepper sauce to taste
2 1-pint canning jars and lids, sterilized

Place ingredients in a heavy saucepan; bring to a boil. Reduce heat; simmer until thickened and reduced in half. Remove from heat; divide equally and pour sterilized jars. Seal with lids; process in a boiling water bath for 10 minutes. Set jars aside until cool to touch; press on lids to check for seals. Make 2 jars.

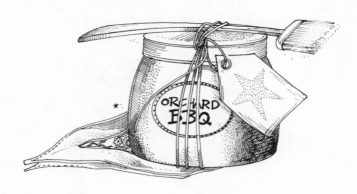

Tie a small baster brush onto a jar of
Orchard Barbecue Sauce...slip inside the pocket of a
new apron and give to your favorite outdoor chef.

Chicken Spice Coating Mix

Store in an airtight container in the freezer for up to 12 months.

1 c. bread crumbs
1/2 c. all-purpose flour
2 t. dried, minced onion
2 t. dried, minced celery
2 t. poultry seasoning

1 t. garlic powder
1 t. paprika
1/2 t. cayenne pepper
1/2 t. onion salt
1/2 t. pepper

Combine ingredients; store in an airtight container. Attach instructions. Makes about 2 cups.

Instructions:

Blend 1/2 cup milk and one egg together in a pie pan; set aside. Rinse and pat 4 boneless, skinless chicken breasts; set aside. Add one cup coating mix to a small bag; set aside. Dip chicken breasts into milk mixture; add to coating mix, shaking to cover. Arrange chicken in a greased casserole dish; bake at 375 degrees until juices run clear when chicken is pierced with a fork, about one hour. Serves 4.

Chicken Spice Coating Mix makes enough for 2 meals, so invite friends over for a chicken dinner made with half the mix, then send them home with the other half...they'll love it!

Italian Coating Mix

Just shake it up and bake!

4 c. fine bread crumbs
1/2 c. grated Parmesan cheese
1/2 c. oil
3 cloves garlic, minced

1 c. fresh parsley, chopped
1 t. dried oregano
1 t. salt
1 t. pepper

Combine ingredients in an airtight container; attach instructions. Store in refrigerator up to one week. Makes about 6 cups.

Instructions:

Place 1-1/3 cups mix in a plastic zipping bag; add 2-1/2 pounds chicken, a few pieces at a time to the mix. Shake to coat; arrange in a greased 13"x9" baking pan. Bake at 400 degrees for 40 minutes or until juices run clear when chicken is pierced with a fork. Serves 4 to 6.

Give Italian Coating Mix with a jar of pasta sauce and a package of spaghetti noodles. Add a line to the instructions: "Pour sauce over chicken during the last 10 minutes of baking; serve over cooked spaghetti."

Cheese & Macaroni Sauce Mix

This mix also makes a tasty nacho dip by stirring the prepared cheese sauce with a jar of salsa...or mix with broccoli for a cheesy baked potato topping.

4-1/2 c. dehydrated cheese
    sauce mix
2-2/3 c. powdered milk
2-2/3 c. dehydrated butter
    powder

2-2/3 c. all-purpose flour
2 t. onion powder
1 t. salt

Combine ingredients; store in an airtight container. Attach instructions. Makes about 12-1/2 cups.

Instructions:

Whisk 1/2 cup sauce mix with one cup hot water in a saucepan; bring to a boil, stirring often. Remove from heat; stir into 4 cups cooked elbow macaroni. Makes 8 servings.

Give a busy mom Cheese & Macaroni Sauce Mix. Make it extra special by slipping a package of elbow macaroni inside a grater, then tie the mix and a wedge of cheese on top.

Alfredo Sauce Mix

Stir cooked chicken and mushrooms into prepared pasta for an easy meal the whole family will love.

2 c. powdered milk
1 c. all-purpose flour
2 t. salt

1/4 t. white pepper
1 c. chilled butter

Combine milk, flour and salt; cut in butter with a pastry cutter until fine crumbs form. Refrigerate in an airtight container; attach instructions. Makes about 3 cups.

Instructions:

Mix 1/4 cup mix, 1/2 cup water, salt and pepper to taste in a small saucepan; heat thoroughly, stirring until creamy. Pour over one pound cooked, hot pasta; toss with with 4 minced garlic cloves, one cup grated Romano cheese and one cup light cream. Serve immediately. Serves 6 to 8.

ALFReDo SAUCe MiX

Mix ¼ cup mix, ½ cup water, salt & pepper to taste in a small saucepan; heat thoroughly, stirring until creamy. Pour over 1 lb. cooked, hot pasta; toss with 4 minced garlic cloves, 1 cup grated romano cheese & 1 cup light cream. Serve immediately.

Here's your instruction tag to copy & tie on.

Ranch Dressing Mix

Delicious over fresh salads or used as a dip for bite-size veggies.

15 saltine crackers
1 c. dried parsley
1/2 c. dried, minced onion
2 T. dried thyme
1/2 T. pepper

1/2 t. garlic salt
1/2 t. onion salt
1/2 t. garlic powder
1/2 t. onion powder

Blend crackers in a blender into fine crumbs; mix in remaining ingredients. Place in an airtight container; attach instructions. Makes about 2 cups.

Instructions:

Whisk one cup mayonnaise, one cup buttermilk and one tablespoon Ranch Dressing Mix together; refrigerate until chilled. Makes 2 cups.

A gardener's delight! Fill a large terra cotta pot with a trowel, garden markers, seed starter mix, gardening gloves and a new gardening magazine...toss in a package of Ranch Dressing Mix and seed packets for tomatoes, lettuce and carrots.

Herb Salad Dressing Spice Mix

Who wouldn't love to have this mix in the pantry?

1/4 c. dried parsley
2 T. dried oregano
2 T. dried basil
2 T. dried marjoram
2 T. sugar

1 T. fennel seed, crushed
1 T. dry mustard
1 t. pepper
1/2 t. garlic salt

Place ingredients in a 1/2-pint jar; secure lid. Shake to mix; store in a cool, dry cupboard up to six weeks. Attach a instructions. Makes about one cup.

Instructions:

Whisk one tablespoon mix, 3/4 cup water, 3 tablespoons white vinegar, one tablespoon olive oil and one crushed garlic clove together; set aside for 30 minutes for flavors to blend. Makes about one cup.

A sampler seasoning pouch makes a clever gift for cooks.
Lay a square dinner napkin flat, fold three corners to the
center and handstitch together, forming an envelope.
Fill it with several bags of seasoning mix, then fold the
fourth corner down to close. Add a button, or wrap
a ribbon around to secure.

Tasty Taco Seasoning Mix

Use this mix to flavor beef, chicken, soups, meatballs and refried beans.

3/4 c. dried, minced onion
1/4 c. salt
1/4 c. chili powder
1 T. dried oregano
2 T. cornstarch

2 T. red pepper flakes
1 T. garlic powder
2 T. cumin
1 T. onion salt

Combine ingredients in a large plastic zipping bag; close tightly. Shake to mix well. Attach instructions. Makes 2 cups.

Instructions:

Add 2 tablespoons mix to one pound browned ground beef and 1/2 cup water; heat through. Serves 4.

Deliver a package of Tasty Taco Seasoning Mix with fresh toppings like lettuce, tomatoes, onions and a can of refried beans. Include flour tortillas with a fluted mold...friends can make taco salad bowls, by pressing tortillas into mold and baking until crisp!

Olé Spicy Bean Salsa

Delicious with chips or as a taco topper.

15-oz. can black-eyed peas,
  drained and rinsed
15-oz. can black beans, drained
  and rinsed
15-oz. can corn, drained
1/2 c. onion, chopped
1/2 c. green pepper, chopped

4-oz. can diced jalapeño
  peppers, drained
14-1/2 oz. can diced tomatoes,
  drained
1 c. Italian salad dressing
1/4 t. garlic salt

Combine the first 7 ingredients in a mixing bowl; mix well. Stir in
salad dressing and garlic salt. Cover and refrigerate overnight, allowing
flavors to blend. Makes about 2 quarts.

Tuck a jar of Olé Spicy Bean Salsa and a bag of tortilla chips
inside a big sombrero. Add a small piñata filled with
candy...snacks and entertainment in one gift!

Citrus Spice Blend

Use to flavor beef, pork or vegetable dishes.

2 T. dry mustard
2 T. orange zest
1-1/2 T. allspice
1-1/2 T. nutmeg
1-1/2 T. ground ginger

1/8 t. ground cloves
2 t. salt
2 t. pepper
2 t. cayenne pepper

Mix ingredients together; store in an airtight container. Makes about 1/2 cup.

Cooking-Out Steak Rub

A great blend to keep stocked during grilling season...wonderful when generously rubbed over steaks.

1/2 c. brown sugar, packed
1/4 c. sugar
2 T. chili powder
2 T. paprika
1 T. dried oregano
1 T. dried thyme

1 T. dried basil
2 T. dry mustard
1 T. cayenne pepper
2 T. garlic powder
2 T. dried, minced onion

Combine ingredients; store in an airtight container. Makes about 1-1/2 cups.

Backyard fun! Pair grilling spices and blends with citronella candles, Frisbees® and a T-ball set.

Apricot & Almond Chutney

Bursting with flavor!

1 c. cider vinegar, divided
1 c. sugar
12 apricots, pitted and chopped
2 red peppers, chopped
2 onions, chopped
1 clove garlic, chopped
1 orange, seeded and chopped
1 lemon, seeded and chopped

1/2 c. sliced candied ginger, chopped
1/2 t. salt
1/2 c. raisins
1/2 c. chopped almonds
1 t. ground ginger
2 1-pint canning jars and lids, sterilized

Pour 3/4 cup vinegar into a saucepan; add sugar. Stir over low heat until sugar is dissolved; bring mixture to a boil and simmer for 5 minutes. Add fruits, vegetables and candied ginger to sugar mixture; simmer over medium heat for 30 minutes, stirring constantly. Add almonds, ginger and remaining vinegar; simmer 30 additional minutes or until chutney has reduced and thickened. Spoon into warm jars to within 1/2 inch from rims; add lids and seal. Process in a boiling water bath for 10 minutes. Makes 2 jars.

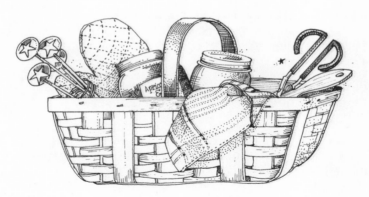

When the temperature rises, treat a friend who loves to cook outdoors to a grilling-themed basket. Stock it with skewers, oven mitts, tongs, tasty condiments and a jar of Apricot & Almond Chutney.

Bacon Dip Spice Packet

*Seal the mix in a small plastic zipping bag and label for a
quick & easy dip mix packet.*

2 T. bacon bits
1 T. dried, minced onion
1 t. beef bouillon granules

1/8 t. dried, minced garlic
1/8 t. dried chives

Combine ingredients; mix well. Place in an airtight container; attach
instructions. Makes about 1/4 cup.

Instructions:

Whisk one cup sour cream and mix together; cover and refrigerate for
at least one hour before serving. Makes one cup.

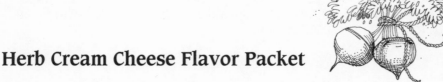

Herb Cream Cheese Flavor Packet

Great with crackers, bagels and fresh veggies.

1/4 c. dill weed
1 T. dried, minced onion
1 t. garlic powder

1 t. dry mustard
1 t. celery seed

Combine ingredients; store in an airtight container. Attach instructions.
Makes about 1/4 cup.

Instructions:

Blend an 8-ounce package softened cream cheese and 1/2 cup butter
together; stir in 2 teaspoons herb mix. Refrigerate until serving. Makes
1-1/2 cups.

YEEHAW

from the kitchen of

1. Copy   2. Color   3. Cut Out!

the **Kitchen maestro's** TOP SECRET seasoning mix *

from:

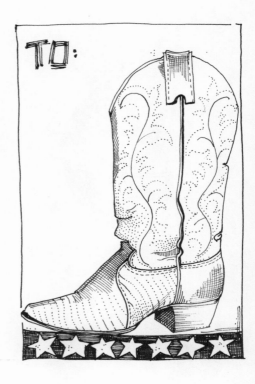

TO:

Give

and it shall be given unto you; good measure; pressed down and shaken together and

RUNNING OVER.

- Luke 6 : 38

from the Kitchen of:

One of the very nicest things about life is the way we must regularly stop whatever it is we are doing and devote our attention to

EATING!

LUCIANO PAVAROTTI

Cut the top of a brown paper bag with decorative edge scissors & fill with a snack mix.

super snack pack!

Deliver a soup mix in a basket filled with toppers...chives, shredded cheese & crackers.

feel better soon!

Soups & Snacks

Use stamps to decorate a canvas bag & fill with mix.

Give a soup mix in an oversized mug or thermos.

Feel-Better Soup Mix

Tie a new speckled ladle onto a soup mix in a jar.

Tortilla Soup Mix in a Jar

Easy to make, flavorful and filling!

2 T. chicken bouillon granules
1 t. lemon pepper
1 t. dried cilantro
1/2 t. garlic powder
1/2 t. cumin
1/2 t. dried oregano
1/2 t. salt

1/4 c. dried, minced onion
1 c. long-grain rice, uncooked
2 to 2-1/2 c. tortilla chips,
   coarsely crushed
5-oz. can chicken
10-oz. can diced tomatoes with
   chiles

Combine the first 8 ingredients in a plastic zipping bag; set aside.
Layer rice in a wide-mouth, one-quart jar; pack seasoning bag on top.
Fill remaining jar with crushed tortilla chips, packing gently; secure lid.
Tape can of chicken to the top of the jar, if desired. Tie jar of mix to the
can of diced tomatoes; attach instructions.

Instructions:

Place tortilla chips in a small bowl; set aside. Remove seasoning
packet; set aside. Add rice to a stockpot; stir in 10 cups water. Mix in
tomatoes with chiles and seasoning packet; bring to a boil. Reduce
heat; simmer for 20 minutes. Add tortilla chips; cover and simmer
5 additional minutes. Spoon into bowls while hot. Makes 3 quarts.

Give Tortilla Soup Mix in a Jar with homemade salsa and a bag
of chips to snack on while the soup's cooking.

soups & snacks

Italian Soup Mix in a Jar

Deliver with a batch of freshly baked bread sticks.

1/2 c. dried pinto beans
1/2 c. dried pink beans
1/2 c. dried kidney beans
1 c. small bowtie pasta,
    uncooked
1 T. dried parsley
1 T. chicken bouillon granules

1 t. dried oregano
1 t. dried basil
1 t. garlic salt
1 t. salt
1/2 t. dried, minced garlic
1/4 t. red pepper flakes

Layer beans in order listed in a one-quart, wide-mouth jar; set aside.
Place pasta in a plastic zipping bag; gently pack on top of beans.
Secure lid; set aside. Toss remaining ingredients together; place
seasonings in a small plastic zipping bag and add to jar. Tie
on instructions.

Instructions:

Set plastic bags to the side; pour beans into a mixing bowl. Rinse with
water; drain. Cover beans with water; let soak overnight. Rinse and
pour into a 5-quart Dutch oven; add 8 cups water, a 28-ounce can
crushed tomatoes, seasoning packet, one cup sliced carrots, one cup
sliced celery and one cup chopped onions. Bring to a boil; reduce heat.
Simmer, covered, for 2 hours; uncover and boil gently until thickened,
about 35 minutes. Stir in pasta; heat until tender, about 10 minutes.
Makes 2 quarts.

Slip a soup mix inside a new thermos and tie on some
mittens...a clever gift for a winter celebration.

Cayenne Cheddar Crackers

Heat 'em up even more by stirring in a few drops of hot pepper sauce or a teaspoon of diced green chiles.

2 c. all-purpose flour
1 t. salt
1/4 t. cayenne pepper
1/4 t. dry mustard

3/4 c. chilled butter
1/2 c. shredded Cheddar cheese
6 to 8 T. cold water

Combine the first 4 ingredients in a mixing bowl; cut in butter with a pastry cutter until coarse crumbs form. Stir in Cheddar cheese and just enough water to hold the dough together; shape into a ball and wrap in plastic wrap. Refrigerate dough for at least 30 minutes. Roll dough out on a lightly floured surface into a 16"x12" rectangle; cut into 3"x1" strips using a sharp knife or pizza cutter. Place on parchment paper-lined baking sheets; bake at 350 degrees for 10 to 12 minutes. Cool; store in airtight containers. Makes 4 dozen.

Use heart, diamond, club and spade cookie cutters to cut out Cayenne Cheddar Crackers...deliver with a package of new playing cards to your favorite bridge partner.

Soups & Snacks

Cup of Veggie Noodle Soup Mix

Keep warm on a chilly day with this cozy treat.

1/3 c. dried mixed vegetable
   flakes
1 T. cracked wheat
2 T. angel hair pasta, coarsely
   broken and uncooked

1/4 t. dried parsley
1/8 t. dried, minced onion
1/4 t. dried basil
1/8 t. garlic powder
1/8 t. onion powder

Blend dried mixed vegetables until flakes smaller than pea-size form in a food processor or electric blender; place in a mixing bowl. Add remaining ingredients; toss to mix well. Divide and place into 2 plastic zipping bags; press to make as airtight as possible. Attach instructions. Makes 2 mixes.

Instructions:

Pour one package soup mix into a bowl or large mug; pour one cup boiling water, chicken broth or beef broth on top. Stir to mix. Makes one serving.

Cup of VEGGIE NOODLE Soup Mix

Pour one package soup mix into a bowl or large mug; pour one cup boiling water, chicken broth or beef broth on top. Stir to mix. Makes 1 serving.

Creamy Cheese Soup Mix

Be sure to give with a package of crackers or homemade bread sticks.

1-1/2 oz. pkg. four cheese sauce
    mix
1 T. chicken bouillon granules
1/2 t. pepper
.9-oz. pkg. vegetable soup mix

1/4 c. dried parsley
3 c. powdered non-dairy creamer
1/4 c. cornstarch
10 plastic zipping bags

Mix ingredients together; place a little less than 1/2 cup mix into
10 separate small jars or plastic zipping bags. Attach instructions.
Makes 10 mixes.

Instructions:

Empty soup mix into a bowl or large mug; stir in one cup boiling
water. Stir until thickened, about 2 to 3 minutes. Makes one serving.

Know someone who's headed off to college? Fill a backpack
with phone cards, stamps, quarters for laundry, pencils, pens,
a family picture and an easy-to-make meal like Creamy Cheese
Soup Mix…it's the next best thing to being home!

soups & snacks

Crispy Parmesan Crackers

Simple to make and outrageously delicious!

1/2 c. butter, softened	1 egg yolk
2 c. all-purpose flour	1/2 c. water
1-1/2 c. grated Parmesan cheese	1 to 2 T. coarse salt

Cut butter into flour with a pastry cutter until coarse crumbs form; mix in cheese and egg yolk. Add enough water to make dough just hold together; divide into 2 portions. Roll dough out on a lightly floured surface to 1/8 to 1/4-inch thickness; cut into small squares using a pizza cutter. Repeat with remaining dough. Sprinkle with coarse salt to taste; arrange on ungreased baking sheets. Prick each cracker 2 or 3 times with the tines of a fork; bake at 350 degrees for 10 minutes. Turn crackers over; bake until golden, about 5 to 10 minutes. Cool completely on wire racks; store in an airtight container. Makes 3 to 4 dozen.

Make gifts extra special with personalized ribbon. Use alphabet stamps, an ink pad made for fabrics and a thin, matte-finish ribbon. Place the ribbon on a paper towel, which will absorb any excess ink, and stamp on initials or names.

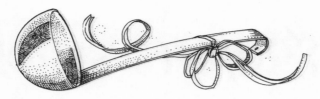

Red Hot Pepper Crackers

Vegetable juice creates a warm color in these snappy crackers.
Try sprinkling with coarse salt or minced garlic before baking.

2 c. all-purpose flour
1/2 t. salt
1/2 t. coarsely ground pepper
1/8 t. cayenne pepper

2 T. butter, softened
2/3 c. plus 1 T. cocktail
  vegetable juice
hot pepper sauce to taste

Combine flour, salt and peppers; cut in butter with a pastry cutter until coarse crumbs form. Set aside. Whisk juice and hot pepper sauce together; mix just enough into the flour mixture so that the dough will hold together. Divide dough in half; roll out by halves on a lightly floured surface to 1/16 to 1/8-inch thickness. Cut into 2-inch squares; arrange on ungreased baking sheets. Prick each 2 or 3 times with the tines of a fork; bake at 325 degrees for 20 to 25 minutes, turning over after 10 minutes. Remove to a wire rack to cool. Makes about 6 dozen.

Welcome a new family to the neighborhood!
Tuck Red Hot Pepper Crackers, a jar of red pepper jelly and a
block of cream cheese inside a basket...be sure to tie a
spreader to the handle.

Soups & Snacks

Mushroom-Barley Soup Mix

You might want to make up several batches...you're sure to get frequent requests!

1/2 c. pearled barley
1/4 c. dried mushroom slices
2 T. dried, minced onion
1/4 c. dried carrot slices
2 T. dried parsley

2 T. dill weed
1/2 t. garlic salt
2 bay leaves
2 t. beef bouillon granules

Combine ingredients in an airtight container; store in a cool, dark cupboard. Attach instructions.

Instructions:

Add mix to one quart boiling water or beef broth; reduce heat and simmer until barley is tender. Remove bay leaves before serving. Makes 4 servings.

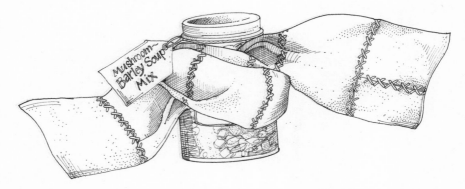

Make a warm scarf out of old wool sweaters in no time. Simply wash them in hot water several times and run them through a hot dryer...this turns the wool into felt. Cut out squares and sew the ends together with chunky yarn to make a patchwork scarf. Wrap around a soup mix and take to a friend on the first day of winter.

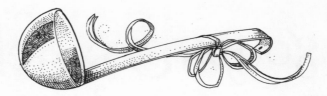

Easy Creamy Potato Soup Mix

Give this mix and you'll be giving comfort!

1/4 c. chicken bouillon granules
3 c. instant mashed potato
   flakes, packed
2 T. dried, minced onion
3 T. dried chives
1 t. white pepper

1/4 c. bacon bits
1 T. dried parsley
1/2 T. dill weed
1/2 t. dried thyme
1 c. powdered milk
1/4 t. paprika

Combine ingredients; mix well. Spoon into a plastic zipping bag. Attach instructions. Makes about 5 cups.

Instructions:

Place 1/2 cup mix into a soup bowl; add one cup boiling water. Stir until smooth and creamy. Makes one serving.

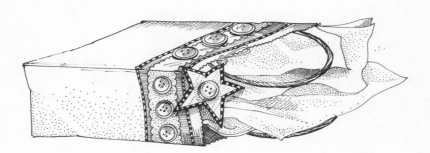

Want to dress up a plain gift bag? Simply glue a length of ribbon around the bag, about one inch from the top. Hot glue a few buttons on the ribbon, slip a soup mix inside and add a homemade gift tag.

Soups & Snacks

Homemade Soup & Salad Croutons

When your friends tell you how tasty these are, don't tell them how simple they were to make!

1 T. butter
5 T. olive oil
2 cloves garlic, minced
1 t. onion salt

1 t. dried thyme
1 t. dried oregano
5 slices day-old bread, crusts
   trimmed

Melt butter with oil in a 12" skillet; mix in the next 4 ingredients. Cube bread; sauté in skillet until golden. Drain croutons on paper towels; cool. Store in an airtight container. Makes 4 servings.

Pick the best from this year's garden...lettuce, cucumbers, tomatoes, onions and radishes. Put them all inside a pretty glass trifle bowl (it's beautiful for serving colorful salads) and add a package of Homemade Soup & Salad Croutons.
A wonderful shower or housewarming gift.

Pistachio Pita Wedges

Delicious with soup and any kind of chip dip.

1 c. pistachios, shells removed
1/2 c. sesame seed
1/2 t. garlic salt

2 8-oz. pkgs. 4-inch pitas, split
   in half horizontally
6 T. olive oil

Finely grind the first 3 ingredients together in a food processor; spread out on wax paper to air dry. Slice each pita round into 4 wedges; brush with olive oil. Sprinkle with nut mixture; press mixture lightly onto wedges using the back of a spoon. Arrange nut-side up on ungreased baking sheets; bake at 425 degrees until golden, about 6 to 8 minutes. Cool on wire racks; store in airtight containers at room temperature. Serves 24.

Next time you're off to a party, take along a Polaroid® camera and a small photo album. Just snap fun candids at the gathering, put them into the album and give to the hostess before leaving!

Soups & Snacks

Gobble-Gobble Turkey Soup Mix

Perfect on a chilly night...so cozy!

1 c. fine egg noodles, uncooked
1-1/2 T. chicken bouillon
   granules
1/2 t. pepper
1/4 t. dried thyme

1/8 t. celery seed
1/8 t. garlic powder
1/8 t. dried basil
1 bay leaf

Combine ingredients; spoon into an airtight jar. Secure lid; attach instructions. Makes about one cup.

Instructions:

Add soup mix and 8 cups water to a large stockpot; mix in one cup diced carrots, one cup diced celery and 1/4 cup diced onion. Bring to a boil; reduce heat, cover and simmer for 15 minutes. Discard bay leaf; stir in 3 cups cooked, chopped turkey. Heat thoroughly, about 15 minutes. Serves 6.

Visiting family or friends on Thanksgiving? Bring a jar of Gobble-Gobble Turkey Soup Mix for your hostess...a great way to use leftover turkey the next day!

10-Minute Rice Mix

Be sure to attach the recipe...they'll definitely want to make this savory side again.

4 c. long-cooking rice, uncooked
1-1/2 oz. pkg. onion soup mix
1/4 c. dried, minced onion
1 T. dried parsley
1/4 t. garlic salt
1/4 t. salt

Combine ingredients; store in an airtight container for up to 4 months. Attach instructions. Makes about 4 cups mix.

Instructions:

Mix one cup mix with 2 cups beef broth in a 2-quart saucepan; add one tablespoon butter. Bring to a rolling boil; reduce heat. Simmer, covered, until liquid is absorbed, about 10 to 15 minutes. Makes 4 servings.

Country Quick & Easy

Pair a package of 10-Minute Rice Mix with a fun kitchen timer and a quick & easy cookbook...friends can make a new tasty meal and add a side of rice in no time!

Soups & Snacks

Bacon-Onion Croutons

Sprinkle these savory croutons into a bowl of soup or toss them in a dinner salad...always delicious.

6 slices French bread, crusts
   trimmed
2 T. bacon drippings
2 T. olive oil

1/2 t. onion powder
1 t. poppy seed
1/2 t. sesame seed, toasted

Cube bread; set aside. Heat remaining ingredients together in a 12" skillet over medium heat; stir in bread cubes until well coated. Remove from heat; spread mixture in a single layer on a rimmed, ungreased baking sheet. Bake at 300 degrees until golden and crisp, about 25 to 30 minutes. Cool. Makes about 2 cups.

Fill a wooden salad bowl with Bacon-Onion Croutons and oodles of tasty salad toppers...sunflower seeds, sun-dried tomatoes, slivered almonds, packages of cheese, red pepper flakes and a bottle of vinegarette. Everyone will have a ball dressing their salads!

Herb Rice Mix

*Use wild rice and add a sprinkling of pine nuts to this mix
for an even heartier side.*

4 c. long-cooking long-grain
   rice, uncooked
1/2 c. powdered milk
1/4 c. dried, minced celery

2 T. dried parsley
2 T. dried thyme
1 T. dried marjoram
1 T dried chives

Combine ingredients; store in an airtight container for up to 4 months.
Attach instructions. Makes 5 cups.

Instructions:

Mix one cup mix with 2 cups chicken broth in a 2-quart saucepan;
add one tablespoon butter. Bring to a rolling boil; reduce heat. Simmer,
covered, until liquid is absorbed, about 10 to 15 minutes. Makes
4 servings.

Tuck several packages of rice mix inside an Oriental take-out
box and toss in a couple fortune cookies. Decorate the outside
with stickers and stamps and slip a pair of chopsticks
under the handle.

Soups & Snacks

Quick Sage Stuffing Mix

A savory side any family will love.

2 t. dried, minced onion
2 t. dried parsley
1 t. dried thyme
1/2 t. garlic powder

1/4 t. dried sage
salt and pepper to taste
8 c. dried bread cubes

Combine ingredients; mix well. Store in an airtight container; attach instructions.

Instructions:

Add 6 tablespoons butter and one cup chicken broth to a large stockpot; heat over low heat until butter melts, stirring frequently. Stir in stuffing mix; mix well. Cover tightly; set aside for 5 minutes. Fluff with a fork before serving. Serves 6.

Give Quick Sage Stuffing Mix along with a personal herb garden...more spices can be added at any time! Just arrange tiny pots of herbs in a small wooden crate and add garden markers to identify each one.

Munch & Crunch Snack Mix

A crunchy snack with a southwestern kick.

1 c. mini pretzels
1 c. corn chips
1 c. oyster crackers
1 c. pumpkin seeds, toasted
1 c. honey-roasted peanuts
2 T. margarine, melted

2 T. brown sugar, packed
1 t. Worcestershire sauce
1 t. chili powder
1/2 t. onion salt
1/2 t. cumin
1/8 t. cayenne pepper

Toss the first 5 ingredients together in a large mixing bowl; set aside. Whisk remaining ingredients together; pour over snack mix, stirring to coat. Spread mix in a roasting pan; bake at 300 degrees for 25 minutes, stirring after 12 minutes. Cool completely; store in an airtight container. Makes about 5 cups.

Bon Voyage! Send off vacationing friends with a road trip gift basket. Include crossword puzzles, playing cards, magazines, juice boxes and Munch & Crunch Snack Mix...add a road map, just in case!

Soups & Snacks

Healthy Day Snack Mix

A good-for-you snack loaded with flavor.

1/2 c. oil
1/2 c. maple syrup
1-1/2 c. brown sugar, packed
6 c. long-cooking oats,
    uncooked
2 c. chopped walnuts

1 c. wheat germ
1 c. flaked coconut
1 c. raisins
1 c. sweetened, dried cranberries
    or cherries

Combine oil, maple syrup and brown sugar in a microwave-safe bowl; heat on high for 3 minutes or until sugar dissolves, stirring often. Set aside. Mix oats, walnuts, wheat germ and coconut in a large mixing bowl; pour syrup mixture on top, stirring well. Spread evenly into 2 buttered 17"x11" rimmed baking pans; bake at 350 degrees for 20 minutes, stirring once halfway through baking. Cool mixture in pans for one hour; sprinkle with raisins and cranberries and mix well. Store in airtight containers up to 2 weeks. Makes about 15 cups.

Fill an athletic water bottle with Healthy Day Snack Mix and deliver with a new workout towel to a favorite fitness friend.

Summertime Corn Dog Mix

Hot diggety good!

1 c. all-purpose flour
2/3 c. cornmeal
1-1/2 t. baking powder

2 T. sugar
2 T. shortening
1/2 t. salt

Combine ingredients; mix well. Store in an airtight container up to 6 weeks. Attach instructions.

Instructions:

Combine mix with one egg and 2/3 cup milk; mix well. Insert one popsicle stick into the end of a hot dog; dip into batter, coating completely. Deep fry until golden; drain on paper towels. Repeat with remaining batter. Makes 12 to 16 servings.

Nothing could be more fun than giving a pair of tickets to an amusement park with Summertime Corn Dog Mix!

Soups & Snacks

Ballpark Peanuts & Popcorn

Just like the old-fashioned ballpark favorite.

5 qts. popped popcorn	2 c. brown sugar, packed
1 c. butter	1/4 t. baking soda
1/2 c. corn syrup	1 t. vanilla extract
1 T. white vinegar	1 c. peanuts

Spread popcorn in a lightly buttered roasting pan; set aside. Bring next 4 ingredients to a boil in a heavy saucepan over medium heat; boil for 5 minutes. Remove from heat; carefully stir in baking soda, vanilla and peanuts. Pour over popcorn; stir to coat. Bake at 250 degrees for one hour, stirring every 15 minutes. Store in an airtight container. Makes about 5 quarts.

Surprise a baseball fan of any age. Tuck a package of Ballpark Peanuts & Popcorn inside a baseball cap...be sure to find out their favorite team. For a really special occasion, include a pair of tickets to the next home game!

Supreme Popcorn-Cracker Mix

Always a winner!

6 c. popped popcorn
2 c. bite-size cheese crackers
1 clove garlic, minced

3/4 t. chili powder
1 T. butter
1/4 t. onion salt

Toss popcorn and cheese crackers together in a large mixing bowl; set aside. Sauté garlic and chili powder in butter until tender; sprinkle with onion salt. Drizzle over popcorn mixture; toss to coat. Makes 6 servings.

All-American Snack Mix

Perfect for the annual Memorial Day picnic.

8 c. popped popcorn
3 T. grated Parmesan cheese
2 c. potato sticks

1-1/2 c. soy nuts
1 c. sweetened, dried cranberries
1/2 c. roasted sunflower seeds

Place popcorn in a large mixing bowl; lightly spray with non-stick vegetable spray. Sprinkle with Parmesan cheese; toss to coat. Mix in remaining ingredients. Makes 12 servings.

Fill a red speckled enamelware pail with
All-American Snack Mix, then tuck in some mini flags
and tote to the 4th of July cookout.

Soups & Snacks

Traditional Party Mix

Share this easy mix at the next neighborhood gathering...you'll come home with an empty pan!

1/2 c. butter
2 T. Worcestershire sauce
3/4 t. garlic powder
1-1/2 t. seasoned salt
1 t. onion powder
1/2 t. celery salt
hot pepper sauce to taste

1 c. mini pretzel sticks
4 c. doughnut-shaped oat cereal
4 c. bite-size crispy wheat or
    bran cereal squares
4 c. bite-size crispy rice or corn
    cereal squares
2 c. mixed nuts

Combine the first 7 ingredients together in a saucepan; heat over low heat, stirring until butter melts. Set aside. Toss remaining ingredients in a large roasting pan; pour butter mixture on top, tossing to coat. Bake at 300 degrees for 45 minutes, stirring every 15 minutes; spread on aluminum foil to cool. Store in an airtight container. Makes 20 cups.

Clear plastic cups come in all sorts of colors
and they make clever containers for snack mixes. Fill several
with different snacks and tie round sheets of cellophane or
netting over top to keep the goodies inside. Place them all in a
basket or wire carrier and take to the party
hostess...everyone will love to sample.

Nutty Sweet & Salty Snack Mix

Craving something salty and sweet? This recipe makes a large batch for giving to friends...and yourself!

1 lb. mixed nuts
2 T. egg white, beaten
2 T. brown sugar, packed
1 t. salt

1/2 t. pepper
1/4 t. cayenne pepper
1/4 t. paprika
1/8 t. garlic powder

Combine nuts and egg white in a large mixing bowl; set aside. Toss remaining ingredients together; sprinkle over nuts, mixing well. Arrange coated nuts in a single layer on a parchment paper-lined baking sheet; bake at 375 degrees until golden, about 15 minutes. Remove from oven; separate nuts with a fork and allow to cool. Store in an airtight container. Makes 8 servings.

Kids going to the baby-sitter's house for the evening? Send them off with a bucket o' fun! Just gather up crayons, balloons, playing cards, silly glasses and joke books and tuck inside a plastic bucket...add a package of Nutty Sweet & Salty Snack Mix and they'll have a ball.

Soup's ON!

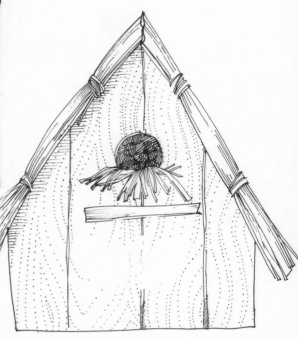

To make
good
soup,
the pot must
only simmer
or
"Smile."

— French proverb

from our house to yours

A little something

good for you

Don't forget to write the instructions on the back!

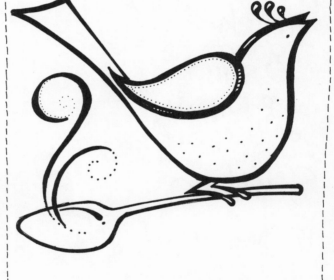

Nothing's better than homemade

Add a bag of mini marshmallows to a cocoa mix.

Tuck a mix inside a sweet little teapot.

Sips & Stirs

cup of friendship

Dip peppermint sticks into chocolate for quick & easy stirrers.

Wax. lined coffee bags are perfect for filling with mocha mixes.

Fill an oversized mug with a coffee mix & office goodies... fun pens, paper clips & sticky notes.

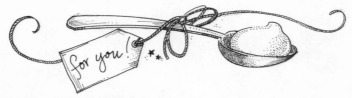

Snickerdoodle Coffee Mix

A tasty treat every coffee-drinking co-worker would appreciate.

1 c. sugar
1 c. powdered milk
1/2 c. vanilla-flavored powdered
   non-dairy creamer

1/2 c. baking cocoa
3 T. instant coffee granules
1/2 t. allspice
1/4 t. cinnamon

Combine ingredients; store in an airtight container. Attach instructions.
Makes about 3 cups.

Instructions:

Add 3 tablespoons mix to 3/4 cup boiling water; stir well. Makes
one serving.

It doesn't get any better than

Snickerdoodle
Coffee Mix

from:
....

Add 3 tablespoons mix to 3/4 cup of
boiling water, stir well. Makes 1 serving.

Here's your instruction tag
to copy & tie on.

Sips & Stirs

Cheery Cherry Hot Cocoa Mix

So much fun to send to friends away from home.

3/4 c. hot chocolate mix   4 cherry-flavored licorice twists
3/4 t. cherry drink mix

Combine first 2 ingredients in a plastic zipping bag; shake to mix. Wrap licorice twists in plastic wrap; attach to mix. Tie on instructions. Makes about one cup.

Instructions:

Add 3 tablespoons mix to 3/4 cup boiling water; stir well with one licorice twist. Makes one serving.

Add some jingle cheer to Cheery Cherry Hot Cocoa Mix. Slip a mix inside a red paper sack, fold the top over and punch holes across the top in one-inch intervals. Thread a large needle with thin ribbon and weave through the holes to close, adding jingle bells along the way.

South Sea Tea Blend

*When the weather turns hot, give this mix with a pitcher
to make sun tea!*

2 c. unsweetened instant tea
2 3-oz. boxes orange-pineapple
   gelatin mix

1 c. sugar
3/4 t. coconut extract
1/8 t. vanilla powder

Combine ingredients in a food processor; blend well. Place in an
airtight container; attach instructions. Makes 3-1/2 cups.

Instructions:

Add 2 tablespoons mix to 3/4 cup boiling water; stir well. Serve warm
or cold. Makes one serving.

Candy Tea Stirrers

Wrap each spoon in cellophane and tie to a tea mix.

2 T. fruit-flavored hard candy,
   crushed

2 T. corn syrup
24 plastic spoons

Line a rimmed baking pan with wax paper; spray with non-stick
vegetable spray. Combine crushed candy and corn syrup in a heavy
saucepan; heat over low heat, stirring frequently, until candy melts.
Spoon mixture into the bowl of each spoon; place spoons on prepared
pan with the handles on the rim so the spoon bowls are level. Set
aside to harden. Store in an airtight container. Makes 24.

Sips & stirs

Relaxing Tea Creamer Mix

*Stirred into tea, this mix creates a delightful Chai-like drink...add a
1/4 teaspoon white pepper for even more spice.*

1 t. cardamom
1 t. sugar
3/4 t. cinnamon
1/2 t. ground cloves

1/2 t. nutmeg
14-oz. can sweetened condensed
milk

Stir ingredients together; cover and refrigerate for at least 24 hours.
Pour into an airtight container and attach instructions. Store in
refrigerator Makes about 2 cups.

Instructions:

Add 2 teaspoons creamer to a cup of brewed strong black tea; stir well.
Makes one serving.

Tea for two! Use a paint pen to write a whimsical quote or
poem around a plain white teapot and fill it with Relaxing Tea
Creamer Mix. Take it along when visiting a friend on a
Saturday afternoon...she'll love it!

Cinnamon Spice Beverage Mix

Friends can skip a visit to the coffeehouse by stirring this mix into a mug of boiling water.

2/3 c. instant coffee granules
1-1/3 c. sugar
1/2 t. cinnamon

1/2 t. nutmeg
1/2 t. allspice
1/8 t. ground cloves

Combine ingredients in a blender; blend to a fine powder. Store in an airtight container; attach instructions. Makes about 2 cups.

Instructions:

Add 2 rounded teaspoons to one cup boiling water; stir well. Makes one serving.

Cinnamon
Spice Beverage Mix

Add 2 rounded teaspoons to 1 cup boiling water, stir well. Makes 1 serving.

Personalized stationery makes a special gift any time of the year. Simply use rubber stamps to add initials or designs on the top of plain paper. Stamp envelopes to match and wrap together with a big satin bow.

Sips & stirs

Warm Sips Spice Bundles

Delightful after a day of fun in the snow.

8 cinnamon sticks, crushed
2 whole nutmegs
1/3 c. whole cloves
2 T. orange zest

2 T. lemon zest
1/4 c. whole allspice
cheesecloth

Combine ingredients in a mixing bowl. Place one tablespoon mixture in the center of a double-thickness 4"x4" square of cheesecloth and tie closed; repeat with remaining mixture. Store in an airtight container before giving; attach instructions. Makes about 15.

Instructions:

Simmer one quart cider or tea with one spice bundle in a large saucepan. Ladle into mugs. Makes 4 servings.

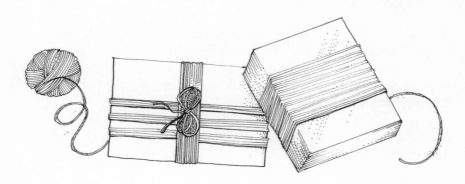

Fill a small box with several Warm Sips Spice Bundles and wrap it up in snowy white paper, topping it off with a bow. Add extra warmth by using yarn in place of ribbon...just wind it around the package several times for thick, fuzzy stripes.

Cappuccino Coffee Creamer

Make this recipe into an instant coffee mix by adding 1/2 cup instant coffee granules...add hot water and enjoy.

3/4 c. powdered non-dairy
   creamer
1 c. hot chocolate mix

1/2 t. cinnamon
1/2 t. nutmeg

Combine ingredients; store in an airtight container. Attach instructions. Makes about 1-3/4 cups.

Instructions:

Stir one to 2 teaspoons into one cup hot coffee. Makes one serving.

Orange Coffee Creamer

To dry orange zest, just spread grated orange peel in a single layer on a pie plate and bake in a 200-degree oven until crisp.

3/4 c. sugar
1 c. powdered milk

1/2 t. orange zest

Combine ingredients; store in an airtight container. Attach instructions. Makes 1-3/4 cups.

Instructions:

Stir one to 2 teaspoons into one cup hot coffee. Makes one serving.

Sips & Stirs

Buttermint Coffee Blend

So creamy and rich!

1/2 c. powdered non-dairy
    creamer
1/2 c. buttermints, coarsely
    crushed
1/4 c. powdered sugar

2 c. powdered milk
3/4 c. instant coffee granules,
    divided
2 1-pint jars and lids

Combine the first 4 ingredients together in medium mixing bowl;
divide equally and pour into jars. Divide and layer instant coffee on
top of each. Secure lid; attach instructions. Makes 2 jars.

Instructions:

Place mixture in a bowl; toss lightly. Spoon back into jar. Combine
1/4 cup mix with 2/3 cup boiling water; stir until mixture dissolves.
Makes one serving.

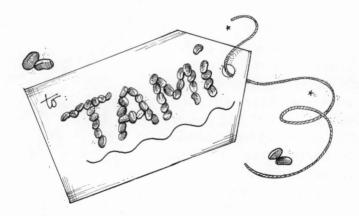

Dress up coffee mix gift tags with coffee beans. Just arrange
them around the gift tag for a border, or use them to spell
out names...very clever!

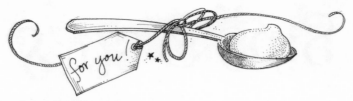

The Sweetest Spoons

Give with a hot chocolate or coffee mix...a heavenly treat!

1 c. chocolate chips	16 to 20 plastic spoons
1 c. butterscotch chips	Optional: colorful sprinkles

Place chocolate chips in a microwave-safe bowl; heat in microwave in 30-second intervals, stirring after each, until melted and smooth. Repeat process in a separate bowl with butterscotch chips. Dip half the spoons in the butterscotch chips to cover the bowl of the spoon; place on wax paper and chill until firm. Dip remaining spoons in chocolate mixture to cover the bowl of the spoon; place on wax paper and chill until firm. Once hardened, dip the chocolate-covered spoons into the butterscotch chips and dip the butterscotch-dipped spoons in the chocolate chips; place on wax paper and sprinkle with colorful sprinkles, if desired. Chill until firm before wrapping individually. Makes 16 to 20.

Friends will love their coffee breaks even more with The Sweetest Spoons! Fill a tin cup or a small vase with coffee beans and insert the spoon handles, so the spoons stand up in the beans. Wrap with clear cellophane, gather ends at the top and tie with a pretty ribbon.

Sips & Stirs

White Hot Cocoa Mix

Present this mix in an old-fashioned milk bottle...so charming!

2 t. vanilla powder
2 t. orange zest

1 c. white chocolate chips
1/4 c. mini marshmallows

Combine ingredients; place in a small airtight container. Attach a gift tag with instructions. Makes about 1-1/4 cups.

Instructions:

Combine 1-1/2 cups milk and 1/4 cup mix in a heavy saucepan over medium heat. Whisk well until chocolate is melted and smooth. Makes one serving.

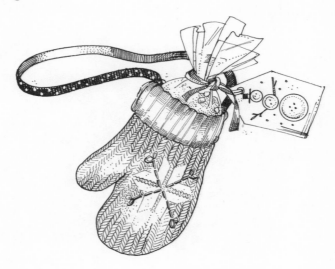

Welcome Winter this year. Sew both ends of a length of ribbon to the cuff of a big woolly mitten. Tuck a container of White Hot Cocoa Mix inside and hang on a neighbor's doorknob after the first snowfall.

Frothy Mocha au Lait Mix

*For variety, mix in a handful of crushed butterscotch, peppermint
or cinnamon candies.*

1-1/2 c. powdered milk
1/3 c. brown sugar, packed
1/2 c. instant coffee granules

3/4 c. mini semi-sweet chocolate
  chips
1/8 t. nutmeg

Combine ingredients; mix well. Spoon into an airtight container; attach
instructions. Makes about 3 cups.

Instructions:

Pour 2/3 cup boiling water into a blender; add 1/4 cup mix. Cover with
lid; blend until frothy. Pour into a mug to serve. Makes one serving.

Visiting friends for the weekend? Bring Frothy Mocha au Lait
Mix along with a box of doughnuts or a freshly baked coffee
cake...a really heartfelt (and tasty!) thank-you for hosting.

Sips & Stirs

Back-by-Popular-Demand Hot Cocoa Mix

So easy to keep on hand year 'round.

2-lb. pkg. chocolate drink mix
16-oz. jar powdered non-dairy
   creamer

1-lb. pkg. powdered sugar
8-oz. pkg. powdered milk
2 c. mini chocolate chips

Combine ingredients; store in an airtight container. Attach instructions. Makes 11 cups.

Instructions:

Stir 3 to 4 heaping tablespoons mix into one cup boiling water until chocolate chips melt. Makes one serving.

Year 'round fun! Purchase a calendar for a friend and fill in special dates and creative "to-do's" throughout the year...eat lots of chocolate on February 21, get a pampering manicure on June 15 or enjoy a good book on the porch swing on September 3rd. Present it on New Year's Day, and she'll treat herself all year long!

Fruity Slush Mix

Give a little summer sunshine with this mix!

4 c. sugar
4 c. water
6-oz. can frozen orange juice
    concentrate, thawed

1/2 c. lemon juice
46-oz. can pineapple juice

Combine sugar and water in a medium saucepan; heat over medium-low heat until sugar is dissolved. Add orange juice concentrate, lemon juice and pineapple juice; stir until well blended. Fill 6 to 7 ice cube trays with mixture; freeze until firm. Remove cubes from trays and store in plastic bags in groups of 8 to 10 cubes. Freeze up to 6 months. Makes about 8 servings.

Instructions:

Fill a glass with frozen cubes; add ginger ale to cover. Let stand 15 minutes and stir before serving. Makes one serving.

A heat-wave rescue! Fill an ice bucket with frozen grapes, then nestle a bag of Fruity Slush Mix inside to keep cold. Friends can have something cold to snack on while sipping their fruity drink.

A TOAST

May the roof over us
never **fall in,**
and may we friends
gathered below
never **fall out.**

— IRISH BLESSING —

HoMeMaDe GooDiES

All iN A DAY'S GriND

Time for a little bit of

Coffee Talk

A little gift from:

Just copy, cut out & color!

A little of what you fancy does you good.

– Marie Lloyd –

to:

from:

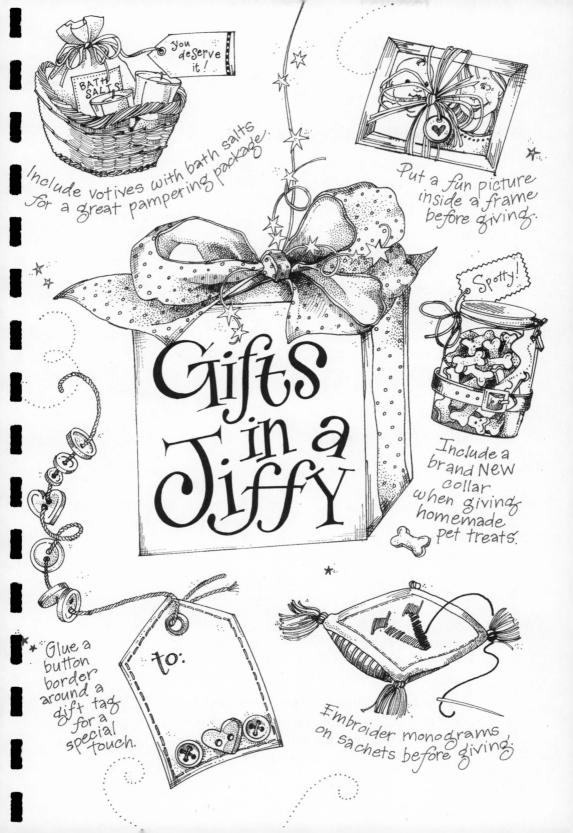

Include votives with bath salts for a great pampering package.

You deserve it!

BATH SALTS

Put a fun picture inside a frame before giving.

Spotty!

Gifts in a Jiffy

Include a brand NEW collar when giving homemade pet treats.

Glue a button border around a gift tag for a special touch.

to:

Embroider monograms on sachets before giving.

Take-it-Easy Bath Crystals

The only thing more relaxing than a warm bath, is a warm bath with these bath crystals!

1 c. sea salt
1 c. Epsom salt
1 c. kosher salt

36 drops lavender essential oil
2 to 3 drops purple food coloring
3 1/2-pint jars and lids

Combine the salts in a plastic zipping bag; add essential oil, shaking bag thoroughly to coat. Add food coloring; shake bag to distribute color. Pour mixture into jars; seal with lids and attach gift tags. Makes 3 jars.

Revitalizing Bath Salts

Luxury in a jar!

2 c. Epsom salts
2 c. coarse salt
20 drops green food coloring
12 drops eucalyptus essential oil

20 drops rosemary essential oil
30 drops peppermint essential
   oil
4 1/2-pint jars and lids

Combine salts in a large mixing bowl; scoop out one cup salt mixture and place in a small mixing bowl. Add food coloring and oils to small mixing bowl; mix well. Pour salt and oil mixture back into large bowl; stir with remaining salt mixture, coating thoroughly. Pour salts into jars; seal lids and attach gift tags. Makes 4 jars.

Looking for supplies to make homemade bath gifts?
Check out craft stores for essential oils and visit the grocery store for Epsom salts and jars.

Gifts in a Jiffy

Homemade Cinnamon-Clove Soap

Individual tart pans make great soap molds too.

4 to 5 empty yogurt cups
1/2 c. clear glycerin soap, cubed
1/2 c. white glycerin soap, cubed

1/4 t. cinnamon
1/4 t. ground cloves

Thoroughly clean yogurt cups; rinse and dry. Lightly coat insides of cups with non-stick vegetable spray; wipe away excess. Place glycerin in a microwave-safe measuring cup and cover top with a paper towel; microwave on medium heat in 25-second intervals until completely melted, making sure not to boil. Stir in cinnamon and cloves, mixing well. Pour soap into prepared yogurt cups to about 1-1/4 inch thickness; Cool and let set for 2 hours; press on sides and bottom to release soap. Allow soaps to cure 3 to 4 weeks before wrapping with clear plastic wrap. Makes 4 to 5 bars.

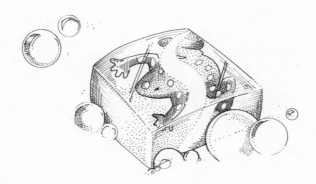

Turn bath time into play time! When making Homemade Cinnamon-Clove soaps for kids, use all clear glycerin, then pour just enough melted soap into yogurt cups to cover the bottom. Place a small toy (a small race car, ring or bracelet) face down inside mold, then pour remaining soap on top. Kids will be scrubbing away to get their treats!

Sunshine Lemon Lip Gloss

Toss a pot into a backpack or lunchbox
on the first (or last!) day of school.

7 to 8 t. almond oil
2 t. beeswax
vitamin E capsule

1 t. honey
5 drops lemon essential oil
4 1/2-oz. lidded pots

Melt oil and beeswax in the microwave in 30-second intervals; add
contents from vitamin E capsule. Whisk in honey and essential oil
until mixture is smooth and almost set. Spoon gloss into pots and
secure lids. Makes 4 pots.

Copy at 100%

Copy and cut out these patterns, then decorate with markers
and glitter...glue them on the lids of Sunshine
Lemon Lip Gloss.

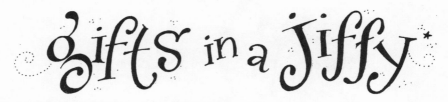

Wintertime Skin Smoother

*When Jack Frost is nipping, this is the perfect gift for
friends & family.*

1/2 c. almond oil
1 oz. beeswax
1 T. cocoa butter
12 drops balsam or peppermint
   essential oil

12 drops vitamin E oil
3 2-oz. jars and lids

Heat almond oil, beeswax and cocoa butter in a double boiler just until
melted; remove from heat. Stir in oils. Pour into jars and secure lids.
Makes 3 jars.

After pulling out the family's coats for winter, tuck a jar of
Wintertime Skin Smoother inside each pocket. It'll be an
unexpected surprise when it's time to bundle up.

Rub-a-Dub Tub "Cookies"

No calories to count with these "cookies"!

2 c. sea salt, finely ground
1/2 c. baking soda
1/2 c. cornstarch
2 T. oil

1 t. vitamin E oil
2 eggs
6 to 7 drops eucalyptus
    essential oil

Combine all ingredients in a mixing bowl until well blended. Roll dough into one-inch balls; place on ungreased baking sheets. Bake at 350 degrees for 10 minutes until golden; cool on wire racks. Store in an airtight container and attach instructions. Makes 2 dozen.

Instructions:

Drop one to 2 "cookies" into a warm bath and allow to dissolve.

Before baking Rub-a-Dub Tub "Cookies," decorate them with anise seeds, cloves or dried orange zest.

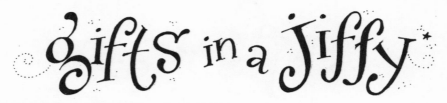
Oatmeal-Honey Body Scrub

Tie a tablespoon onto the jar for easy measuring.

1/4 c. powdered milk
1/4 c. quick-cooking oats,
   uncooked

2 vitamin E capsules
1/4 c. powdered honey
1/4 t. vanilla powder

Place powdered milk in a blender and blend to create a fine powder; set aside. Process oats in a food processor until very fine; add oil from vitamin E capsules and process until well blended. Add powdered milk, powdered honey and vanilla powder; process for 10 to 15 seconds. Pour contents into a one-pint jar; secure lid and attach instructions. Makes about one cup.

Instructions:

Mix one to 2 tablespoons mix with enough water to form a paste. Apply to wet skin in a circular motion. Rinse well with warm water and pat dry.

Gifts for girlfriends! Place a jar of Oatmeal-Honey Body Scrub in the middle of a new fuzzy wash cloth or hand towel. Bring the corners up, secure with a ribbon and tie on a fluffy shower puff.

Simmering Citrus Spice

Friends will love filling their homes with this sweet scent any time of the year.

1 c. cinnamon sticks, broken
 into one-inch pieces
10 drops cinnamon essential oil
1 c. whole allspice
10 drops allspice essential oil
2 c. star anise

1/2 c. coriander seed
2 c. dried orange peel
20 drops orange essential oil
1/2 c. juniper berries
1/2 c. whole cloves
1/2 c. ground nutmeg

Combine cinnamon sticks and cinnamon oil; pour into an airtight container. Combine allspice and allspice oil; layer over cinnamon. Layer anise and coriander seed over top. Combine orange peel and orange oil; pour over ingredients in container. Top with juniper berries, cloves and nutmeg. Secure container lid and shake well. Allow mixture to sit for 2 to 3 days, shaking every 6 to 8 hours. Attach instructions before giving. Makes 8 cups.

Instructions:

Combine one cup spice with 4 cups water in heavy saucepan; bring to a simmer and reduce heat to low. Add water every hour if necessary.

Pamper a busy friend with a vintage pitcher and bowl packed full of herbal bath salts, lotions, soaps, scented votives, flavored tea and a package of Simmering Citrus Spice.

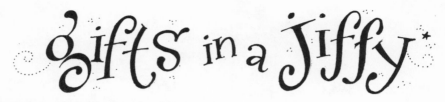

Gifts in a Jiffy*

Refreshing Drawer Sachet

Tie on garden charms before giving to your green-thumb friends...miniature watering cans, trowels and flowers look so sweet.

4 T. dried lavender	3 to 4 drops lemon essential oil
4 T. dried thyme	3 to 4-inch square muslin bag
2 T. lemon balm	Optional: jute and charms

Combine lavender, thyme and lemon balm in a small mixing bowl; crush with the bottom of a drinking glass. Add lemon oil, tossing to mix. Spoon herb mixture into the muslin bag; tie top or sew closed. Decorate with jute and charms, if desired.

Planning to give a quilt or blanket to a friend? Make the gift even more special by adding a secret sachet. Just sew 3 sides of a small square of coordinating fabric onto the quilt to form a pocket, then slip a sachet inside...she'll love to cuddle up with the warm quilt and fresh scent!

Family Recipe Keeper

You might get carried away making separate books for appetizers, main dishes and desserts.

15 to 20 6"x6" squares colored
    paper
hole punch
2 6"x6" squares corrugated
    cardboard

large rubber band
6-inch cinnamon stick
family photo
adhesive spray

Print your favorite family recipes on the colored paper. Punch holes in each recipe page 2 inches from the top and one inch from the left side; repeat hole punching with cardboard squares. Layer the recipe pages between the two pieces of cardboard so the holes align and the corrugated sides are facing the outside. Working from the back of the book, push the end of the rubber band through the top holes using a pencil or skewer; loop the end around the cinnamon stick. Repeat with bottom holes, securing cover and recipes. Secure a family photo on the front with adhesive spray.

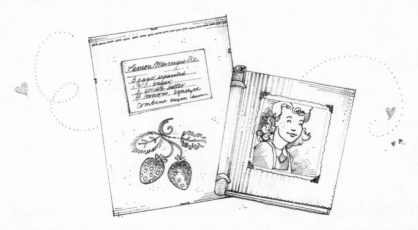

A tribute to Mom! A nostalgic tea towel makes a clever mat for framing Mom's most-treasured recipe. Include a picture of Mom in the kitchen and present with a Family Recipe Keeper.

Gifts in a Jiffy

A Pinch of This Cooking Wreath

The cooks on your gift list will love this. They can use the herbs fresh or after they've dried.

fresh sprigs of parsley
fresh sprigs of thyme
fresh sprigs of oregano
fresh sprigs of marjoram
fresh sprigs of sage
fresh sprigs of basil

fresh sprigs of rosemary
green florists' wire
4 to 5-inch wire wreath form
3 to 4 dried chile peppers
1 garlic bulb

Wrap the stems of each herb bunch with the florists' wire to form 7 bunches. Secure one bunch to the wreath form by twisting florists' wire around the wrapped stems and the wreath. Add a second bunch, so the leaves overlap the stems of the first. Continue around the wreath with remaining bunches. Use wire to attach chile peppers and garlic bulb.

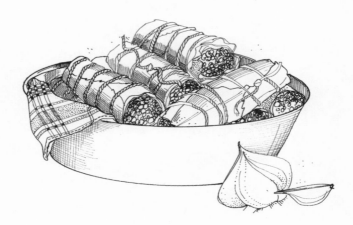

No time to assemble A Pinch of This Cooking Wreath?
Just bundle together all the herb sprigs, wrap fresh bay leaves
around the outside, and secure with several lengths of jute.
So easy!

Home-Sweet-Home Leaf Coasters

A heartfelt gift with nature's touch.

4 4"x4" white ceramic tiles
cotton balls
alcohol
glass paint

4 pressed leaves in varying
　　shapes
1/4-inch wide foil adhesive tape
jute

Wash tiles in soapy water; rinse and dry. Use cotton balls to wipe alcohol over tiles; allow tiles to air-dry. Brush a base color of glass paint on tiles; use different brushes and strokes to create varying textures. Let tiles dry for 15 to 20 minutes. For each tile, brush a contrasting color on a pressed leaf and press over dried base color, creating a different leaf stamp on each tile. Follow tile manufacturer's directions to bake tiles in an oven; cool tiles and apply foil tape around the edges. Stack and wrap with jute.

What a gift! Pair Home-Sweet-Home Leaf Coasters with coordinating mugs...slip a beverage mix inside and wrap it all up with leaf-printed paper.

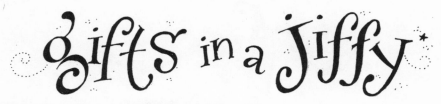

Cheery Stamped Bulletin Board

Teachers, moms and neighbors will love it!

craft glue
8 to 10 round craft buttons
8 to 10 flat silver thumbtacks
flower rubber stamps

stamp pads in coordinating
 colors
24"x18" bulletin board
yellow gingham ribbon

Glue buttons to the flat surface of thumbtacks; set aside. Stamp the flower stamps in stamp pads and stamp 8 to 10 images on bulletin board in desired pattern; allow to dry completely. Add button thumbtacks to the center of each flower. Glue gingham ribbon around the edges of the bulletin board.

Use a paint pen to add a clever saying or quote to a Cheery Stamped Bulletin Board. Give it to teenagers, teachers or a friend starting a new job...be sure to add a colorful note pad and a new pen.

Picture-Perfect Marble Magnets

*You only need 5 minutes to make this fun, simple gift.
After mastering the magnets, try gluing marble pictures to
hair clips, push pins or gift tags!*

1/2-inch circle hole punch
small pictures and patterned
    paper
toothpick

silicone glue
1/2-inch dia. round magnets
1/2-inch dia. clear flat glass
    marbles

Use the hole punch to cut out various designs from pictures and paper.
Use a toothpick to spread a thin layer of silicone glue on a magnet;
place a cut-out over top. Use toothpick again to drop a small amount
of glue onto the center of the picture; lower a marble down over the
glue, being sure to press out any bubbles. Repeat with remaining
magnets and marbles. Allow to dry overnight.

It's so easy! Use alphabet stamps to spell out a friend's name
on scrapbook paper, then make each letter into a
Picture-Perfect Marble Magnet. Give them in a small tin or
attach them onto a galvanized pail filled with flowers...no
need for a gift tag!

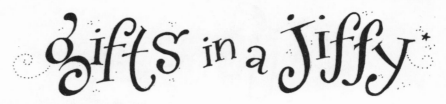

Gifts in a Jiffy

Felt Photo Boxes

Keeps photos organized and safe without spending oodles of time on an album.

brown square paper maché box
black felt
spray adhesive

gold or silver felt
photo

Remove lid from box; set aside. Wrap the box with black felt, covering all areas; use spray adhesive to secure. Cover lid of box with gold or silver felt, attaching with spray adhesive. Replace lid on box. Spray back of photo with adhesive and center on the lid, pressing to secure. Cut a piece of sliver or gold felt so it is one inch smaller that the lid; cut out the center of the felt, so the picture can show through. Attach to lid with spray adhesive so that the photo is framed.

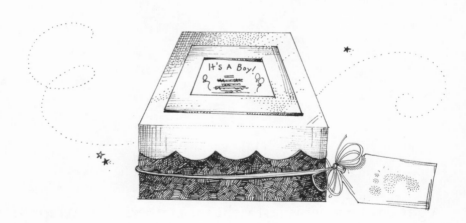

Perfect for new parents! Fill a Felt Photo Box with a couple disposable cameras and add a gift certificate to have pictures developed...place the birth announcement on the lid instead of a photo.

Portrait Notecards

A special card for engagements, weddings and anniversaries.

cardstock
color photo and a black & white
   copy of photo
colored pencils

spray adhesive
1/4-inch wide satin ribbon
hot glue

Fold cardstock in half and trim to create a notecard of desired size. Use the color photograph as a guide to hand-color the black and white copy with colored pencils, using loose diagonal strokes. Crop the colored photo to desired size and attach it to the front of the notecard using spray adhesive. Cut lengths of ribbon to create a frame around the photo and hot glue to notecard. Allow to dry overnight.

A gift-box bouquet is just right for Mothers' Day. Wrap the bottom of a box with pretty paper and fill it with tissue paper that sticks up over the edge to look like an opened gift. Slip a plastic container inside and fill it with well-soaked floral foam. Tuck roses or daisies into the foam, and arrange moss around the stems. Be sure to tie on a Portrait Notecard featuring a favorite photo of the two of you together.

Gifts in a Jiffy

Oh-So-Clever Pajama Bag

Give with a new pair of pj's inside...hang on a bedpost or doorknob!

standard pillow case
2 yards 1-inch wide ribbon
straight pins

needle
thread
Optional: fabric paints

Turn pillow case inside out and lay on a flat surface; lay the ribbon 2 inches from the top of the open end, all the way around the pillow case, leaving the ends at one stitched end of the pillow case. Fold the top of the pillow case over the ribbon; pin the fabric of the pillow case together being sure not to pin the ribbon. Starting at one of the ends of ribbon, use a needle and thread to stitch the pillow case together along the pins. Turn pillow case right-side out. Pull the ends of the ribbon and tie in a bow to form a drawstring bag.

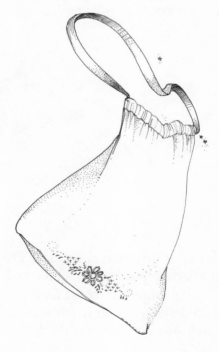

Fill an Oh-So-Clever Pajama Bag with fun...girls headed off to their first slumber party will love it! A new pair of flannel pj's, magazines, some nail polish and stickers will fit nicely inside. Toss in a few packets of cocoa and some homemade cookies for a midnight snack.

Whimsical Ribbon Tray

Ribbons come in so many different colors and patterns...make a tray for every season!

11"x14" wooden frame
cardboard
acrylic paint
assorted ribbons

decoupage medium
2 drawer pulls
drill
screws

Remove backing and glass from frame; set aside. Cut cardboard to just fit inside the frame. Paint frame in desired color; allow to dry completely. Cut assorted ribbons to fit across the width of the cardboard. Working in small strips, paint decoupage medium onto the cardboard; lay a ribbon in place and press firmly. Continue this process until the cardboard is filled with ribbon; let dry. Center drawer pulls on the two, 11-inch sides of the frame; use drill to screw into place to form the handles of the tray. Replace glass; insert cardboard with ribbon so ribbon is showing through glass and secure backing.

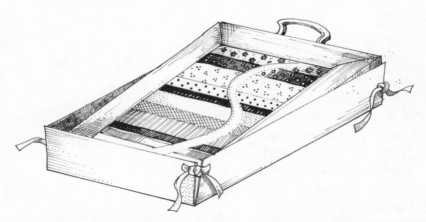

Wrap a Whimsical Ribbon Tray in a handmade gift box. Measure 2 pieces of cardboard so they are 8 inches longer and wider than the tray. Cut 3-inch squares from each corner, and fold sides up to form a box. Thread satin ribbon through holes punched in each side and tie a bow in every corner!

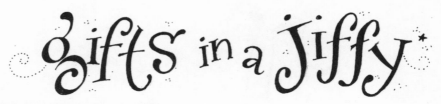

gifts in a Jiffy

Paperwhite Bulb Kit

Give a garden any time of the year.

4-inch dia. terra cotta pot and
   saucer
white and blue acrylic paint
stencil of initial
tape

indoor stain varnish
small rocks and pebbles
paperwhite bulb
satin ribbon

Paint the sides of the terra cotta pot white, without painting the rim;
allow to dry completely. Place the saucer, bottom-side up, on a flat
surface; paint the center area white without painting the rim; let dry.
Apply 2 more coats of white paint to pot and saucer, letting dry
between coats. Center stencil on the side of the pot and tape to secure;
use blue paint to fill in stencil. Carefully remove stencil to reveal the
blue initial on the white paint; let dry. Use blue paint to write a
greeting on the white part of the saucer. Pour rocks and pebbles into
the pot up to the bottom edge of the rim; place the bulb, root-end
down, on the rocks. Fit the saucer, painted-side up, on top of the pot.
Wrap ribbon around the saucer and pot to secure; tie in a bow on top.

Look in gardening magazines for pictures of paperwhites...cut
them out, glue them on cardstock and use as gift tags for
Paperwhite Bulb Kits. Be sure to include your favorite
growing tips on the back!

Journal in a Jar

Jump-start journal writers with this clever gift in a jar.

colorful paper
stickers
markers

clear jar or container
Optional: ribbon and silk flowers

Cut paper into 5"x1" strips of paper. Decorate strips with stickers and use markers to write journal entry questions on the strips. Some questions may be, "What was your favorite childhood memory?" "What do you like most about summertime?" or "What's your mom's favorite piece of advice?" After creating as many questions as desired, fold the strips of paper several times and place in the jar or container. Secure lid; tie a ribbon around the top and glue silk flowers on the lid, if desired. Attach a gift tag with instructions:

Instructions:

Each day, pull out a journal question; paste it to the top of a new journal page and fill in your thoughts.

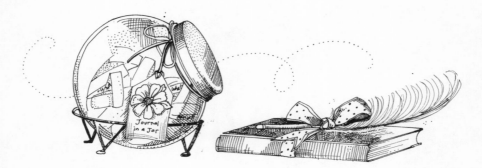

Just right for recent graduates! Pair a Journal in a Jar
with a new blank journal...write a special wish inside and
tie on a fun feather pen.

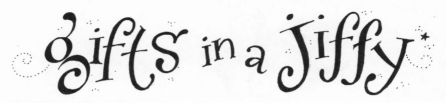

Gifts in a Jiffy

Keepsake Frame

A picture is worth a thousand words…but a picture surrounded by hand-written messages is priceless.

decorative pens
stickers
16"x14" mat with a
    5"x7" opening

16"x14" frame
5"x7" photo
tape

Use pens and stickers to decorate the mat with quotes, pictures and wishes. Remove backing from frame; place decorated mat into frame. Line photo up behind frame, making sure the picture can be seen through the opening; tape to secure. Replace frame backing.

Make a mini Keepsake Frame! Cut a piece of kraft paper to fit inside a clear CD case, glue a picture in the center and decorate the border with fun stickers and messages. Tuck the photo in the inside grooves of the CD cover, so the picture shows on the outside…the frame can stand up on its own by leaving the case open a bit and placing on a flat surface.

Traditional Cinnamon Ornaments

A new recipe for an old-fashioned favorite.

3/4 c. applesauce
1 env. unflavored gelatin mix
1.9-oz. jar cinnamon

1/4 c. cornstarch
3 T. ground cloves
jute

Combine applesauce and gelatin mix in a small saucepan and let stand for 3 minutes. Heat over medium heat until simmering, stirring constantly; remove from heat. Combine cinnamon, cornstarch and cloves in a mixing bowl; stir in applesauce mixture. Turn dough out onto a flat surface and knead 6 to 8 strokes. Divide dough in half and roll each half between sheets of plastic wrap to 1/4-inch thickness. Remove plastic wrap and use cookie cutters to cut out ornaments. Use a drinking straw to cut out holes in the tops of ornaments for hanging. Dry on wire racks overnight. String on jute. Makes 2 dozen.

Make simple gift tags by using alphabet cookie cutters when making Traditional Cinnamon Ornaments. Just cut out initials, let dry, thread jute through holes and tie onto packages. Try decorating with paint, glitter, tiny beads or buttons.

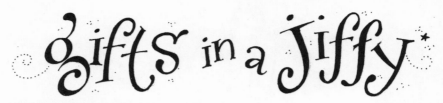

Gifts in a Jiffy

Snowball Gift Package

Make an impression at your next holiday gift exchange with this fun packaging idea...fill snowballs with stickers, gel pens, ornaments or jewelry.

2 c. craft glue
1 c. warm water
white crepe paper

3 to 4 balloons
needle
spray glitter

Mix glue and water in a small bowl to form a paste. Tear paper into 4"x1" strips. Blow up balloons to desired size; tie closed and set knotted end of balloons into cups or mugs in order to work easily with the round surfaces. Dip paper strips into paste and place on balloons covering the entire surface of each balloon, overlapping the strips. Leave the area around the knots uncovered. Let first layer dry for 24 hours. Repeat process adding 2 to 3 more layers. Once last layer is dry, pop balloons with needle and pull out of the openings. Insert shredded paper or cellophane inside each snowball and add the gift. Cover the opening in each ball with layers of paper maché as before to fill in the hole. Once snowballs are completely dry, use spray glitter to cover the outside of each. Makes 3 to 4 packages.

Make Snowball Gift Packages using pink crepe paper and fill it with sparkly hair clips, a pink tulle scarf, stretchy white gloves and baby pink nail polish...a sweet dress-up gift for a little girl.

Tweet Treats

Your feathered friends will thank you.

2 eggs
1/4 c. walnuts
1/4 c. raisins
18-oz. pkg. cornbread mix

1/3 c. apple juice
1/4 c. applesauce
1 c. frozen mixed vegetables,
    thawed

Place eggs, walnuts and raisins in a blender; blend for 5 to 7 seconds.
Place mixture in a mixing bowl; stir in remaining ingredients until
well blended. Pour mixture into a greased 8"x8" baking pan; bake at
400 degrees for 20 minutes. Cool on a wire rack for 10 minutes;
remove from pan to cool completely. Cut into small squares. Makes
3 to 4 dozen.

Surprise bird watchers with a basket full of Tweet Treats
and easy-to-make bird feeders. Simply scoop out an orange
half and thread jute through holes made with a toothpick on
each side. Tie the ends together to make a hanger, then fill
the orange half with dried cranberries and sunflower seeds.

Gifts in a Jiffy*

Dog-Gone-Good Doggie Cookies

Just right for man's best friend.

2 c. mashed potatoes
2 c. milk
1 c. chicken broth
2 c. crunchy peanut butter
1 pkg. active dry yeast
1/2 c. warm water

3 eggs
3-1/2 c. all-purpose flour
2 c. whole-wheat flour
1 c. rye flour
1 c. cornmeal

Mix first 4 ingredients together in a saucepan; bring to a boil, stirring constantly. Remove from heat and cool to room temperature. Dissolve yeast in warm water; add to peanut butter mixture. Blend in eggs until smooth. Gradually mix in flours and cornmeal to form a dough; knead well. Roll dough out to 1/4-inch thickness and place on a greased baking sheet; use a knife to score into squares. Bake at 300 degrees for 45 minutes. Turn oven off, leaving cookies inside overnight. Break into small pieces. Makes 3 to 4 dozen.

Here-Kitty-Kitty Cookies

Purr-fect!

1 pkg. active dry yeast
1/4 c. warm water
1 c. all-purpose flour
1 env. unflavored gelatin mix
1 c. powdered milk

1/4 c. corn oil
1 egg
6-oz. can tuna
1/4 c. water

Dissolve yeast in warm water; set aside. Combine flour, gelatin mix and powdered milk in a mixing bowl; stir in yeast, oil, egg, tuna and water. Stir until well blended. Drop dough by 1/2 teaspoonfuls onto ungreased baking sheets. Bake at 300 degrees for 25 minutes. Cool completely and store in refrigerator. Makes 8 to 10 dozen.

Just copy these tags, color with markers & tie on. So easy!

Enjoy!

from the kitchen of

Use these tags to add a little
whimsy to your gifts.
How fun!

Index

Breads, Spreads & Muffins

Brownies & Bars

Cakes, Pies & More

Index

Index

We've cooked up a whole collection of Gooseberry Patch® books!

Have a taste for more? Call us toll-free at

1-800-854-6673

We'll send you our latest catalog filled with snowmen, Santas, ornaments, candles, cookie cutters, gourmet goodies, calendars, giftwrap, pottery, collectibles and MORE...including our best-selling cookbooks!

Phone us:
1·800·854·6673

Fax us:
1·740·363·7225

Visit our website.
www.gooseberrypatch.com

Send us your favorite recipe!

Include the memory that makes it special for you too!* If we select your recipe for a brand new **Gooseberry Patch** cookbook, your name will appear right along with it...and you'll receive a FREE copy of the book! Mail to:

Vickie & Jo Ann
Gooseberry Patch, Dept. Book
600 London Road
Delaware, Ohio 43015

*Please include the number of servings and all other necessary information!

cups of kindness · kitchen mixes · making memories ♥ surprise ☆! handmade gift tags ♥ sweet treats ♥ quick & clever ✿ thoughtful

yummy recipes

stickers, bows & buttons

special delivery ★ stickers, bows & buttons

Finishing touches · merry making ★ from the heart ·